Complete Conditioning for
Soccer

Sigi Schmid
Bob Alejo

Human Kinetics

Library of Congress Cataloging-in-Publication Data

Schmid, Sigi.
    Complete conditioning for soccer / Sigi Schmid, Bob Alejo.
       p. cm.
    ISBN 0-88011-829-6
    1. Soccer--Training. I. Alejo, Bob, 1957- II. Title.

    GV943.9.T7 S33 2002
    613.7'11--dc21

                                                                                            2001051638

ISBN: 0-88011-829-6

Developmental Editor: Cassandra Mitchell
Assistant Editor: Dan Brachtesende
Copyeditor: Bob Replinger
Proofreader: Erin Cler
Permission Manager: Toni Harte
Graphic Designer: Stuart Cartwright
Graphic Artist: Francine Hamerski
Photo Managers: Tom Roberts and Carl Johnson
Cover Designer: Jack W. Davis
Photographer (cover): Allsport USA
Photographer (interior): Tom Roberts, unless otherwise noted; © Sport the library/Chris Kuputanellis/ Action Photographics 4; © W. Crane 8, 58; © Bongarts 61, 115; © Bongarts/Maring Rose 96; © iphotonews.com/Brooks 119; © The Sporting Image 132; © Essy Ghavameddini/LA Galazy 183
Art Manager: Carl Johnson
Illustrator: Tom Roberts
Printer: United Graphics

Human Kinetics books are available at special discounts for bulk purchase. Special editions or book excerpts can also be created to specification. For details, contact the Special Sales Manager at Human Kinetics.

Printed in the United States of America   10 9 8 7 6 5 4 3 2 1

Human Kinetics

Web site: www.humankinetics.com

United States: Human Kinetics
P.O. Box 5076
Champaign, IL 61825-5076
800-747-4457
e-mail: humank@hkusa.com

Canada: Human Kinetics
475 Devonshire Road Unit 100
Windsor, ON N8Y 2L5
800-465-7301 (in Canada only)
e-mail: orders@hkcanada.com

Europe: Human Kinetics
Units C2/C3 Wira Business Park

West Park Ring Road
Leeds LS16 6EB, United Kingdom
+44 (0) 113 278 1708
e-mail: hk@hkeurope.com

Australia: Human Kinetics
57A Price Avenue
Lower Mitcham, South Australia 5062
08 8277 1555
e-mail: liahka@senet.com.au

New Zealand: Human Kinetics
P.O. Box 105-231, Auckland Central
09-523-3462
e-mail: hkp@ihug.co.nz

CONTENTS

ACKNOWLEDGMENTS

My thanks go to Sigi Schmid for the freedom and independence he allowed me when working with his teams.

UCLA Soccer, 1984–1993, taught me to love a great sport.

Carmella Gutierrez taught me to write. She has my heart and soul.

My daughter, Brianna, is my daily joy.

My career has been blessed by all the athletes I've coached and all the coaches I've worked with. I've learned something from each of them.

Bob Alejo

CHAPTER 1

FITNESS DEMANDS FOR SOCCER

When watching the World Cup unfold on a daily basis, the soccer outsider finds it difficult to feel the intensity of the movements performed during a match. The top players in the world battle one another in what looks like graceful ease rather than laborious effort.

These players make the game of soccer look natural only because they have developed a physical base that allows them to execute perfect volleys, explosive sprints, aggressive marking, and violent shots on goal throughout an entire match.

Many players in the world can kick a ball exactly where they want it to go or keep an attacker from moving past them, but only some of them have the sport-specific skills and the level of conditioning to perform those skills for over 90 minutes.

In other words, possessing strength, power, speed, agility, and endurance is the key to being the best. *Complete Conditioning for Soccer* will give the soccer athlete the opportunity to develop physically to the greatest level possible.

BUILDING THE FOUNDATION

Let's take a brief look at all the components of a good soccer conditioning program.

Flexibility

Flexibility is a basic need for the soccer athlete. Flexibility means having a generous range of motion about a joint. Players achieve flexibility by increasing the elasticity of the muscle or the connective tissue associated with that joint.

Players need a certain amount of flexibility to perform certain soccer movements correctly. Making slide tackles, kicking long volleys, and jumping correctly require the athlete to be flexible. Flexibility also reduces the chance for injury when the body is placed in awkward positions, such as landing on the ground following contact. Although there is a limit to flexibility that protects joints and muscles, a certain range of motion about the joints allows an athlete to achieve positions of greater leverage while sprinting, defending, and striking. When combined with a thorough warm-up, stretching for flexibility can significantly reduce the chance for injury. Chapter 2 will explain the role of flexibility and stretching in more detail.

Strength

The ability of muscles to contract and overcome resistance is an exhibition of strength. Maximal strength is an all-out effort to overcome a maximum resistance, independent of time. Strength in general is the means to achieve the optimal levels of power, endurance, and speed. The development of strength is critical for laying the foundation to perform work specific to soccer. The athlete must develop adequate strength to attempt the type of training designed to increase speed, vertical jump, and endurance.

Examples of the application of strength in soccer are keeping attackers off the ball through better leverage, positioning for balls in the air while maintaining position in a group, and increasing striking velocity through greater leg strength. The speed of Cobi Jones, a premier U.S. soccer player, results from his developing leg strength specific to the game. Following the guidelines in chapter 3 will help you put together a great strength training program specifically for soccer.

Power

The combination of speed and strength is common to successful soccer players. Power is the term applied when speed and strength come together as a unit. The striking, tackling, jumping, and sprinting abilities of Brian McBride are examples of power. The development of a good strength base is the avenue for increasing power. Pure strength alone is too slow for the dynamic sport of soccer, and top speed is momentary without being strong. The soccer athlete must strive to achieve the best combination of both. The discussion in chapter 4 shows how the two can exist in the correct form.

Endurance

The endurance of a soccer athlete is more than just being able to run forever. Speed-endurance, strength-endurance, and power-endurance are three important areas of fitness. Soccer players must have both a high level of running endurance and the ability to run repeatedly at top speeds without much rest. Changing speed and direction is also an example of speed-endurance. The constant pushing and shoving during a match can sap the energy from a defender who lacks strength-endurance. Frequent jumping, tackling, and striking require a certain amount of power-endurance if the athlete is to remain effective for an entire match.

A high level of endurance will allow the soccer athlete to maintain nearly perfect execution of skills at close to 100 percent effort throughout a match. Endurance training is covered in chapter 5.

Agility

The ability to adjust movement quickly based on a changing environment is agility. Because situations develop so rapidly in soccer, the athlete must improvise and swiftly change direction and speed. Making quick decisions and immediately acting on them while moving at game speed could be the difference between scoring or being scored on! The feet, eyes, legs, and brain must be agile and work together if the soccer athlete expects to be successful. Agility is covered in more detail in chapter 6.

Speed

When we speak of speed, typically we think of running fast. But speed in soccer includes much more than just running fast. Quickness, short

bursts of movement, rapid movement in all directions, the ability to start and stop rapidly, speed of reaction time—these are all examples of game speed. Speed is a combination of strength and excellent endurance. Repeatedly moving with 100 percent effort at 100 percent speed requires endurance and strength that the athlete can realize only through specific training. Chapter 7 will explain the training and methods behind increasing speed.

Nutrition

Training would be largely pointless if the foods the athlete eats detract from future efforts toward fitness. Abundant nutritional information is available to today's athlete. Books devoted solely to nutrition are definitely worth looking into. Although this book is about the total conditioning of individuals and teams, space permits only a brief discussion of the important role of nutrition.

In looking at sporting disciplines from bodybuilding to kayaking, it appears that nutrition is the last frontier. Training programs abound, but exercises and methods have remained somewhat unchanged. Nutritional information is turning over rapidly. Researchers are looking more closely at proteins, carbohydrates, fats, minerals, vitamins, and even herbs. They have found interesting and positive results useful to all athletes. Part of nutrition is hydration, the maintenance of fluids in the body. Sports drinks and, more important, water are essential for maintaining body temperature and regulating body functions before, during, and after matches. Players can pass out (or worse!) from lack of hydration.

Good nutritional habits can bring about significant increases in performance. In the past, the right balance of food groups and calories was addressed only at pregame meals. Now we know that a year-round commitment to soccer includes a constant effort toward nutrition. It makes good sense.

The soccer player has specific, nutritional needs unlike those of the general population. The yearly training cycle described in this book demands that players develop good nutritional habits.

A chapter devoted to nutrition would not provide all the information necessary for this topic. You are encouraged to seek sources that focus on nutritional information for athletes.

TRAINING PRINCIPLES

Designing a successful conditioning program is more than just developing all these components of fitness. You need to learn how best to put them together into a training proram. There are two key principles of a good training program —periodization and specificity.

Periodization

Athletes know what kind of result they want from a training program. Through year-round testing and evaluation, athletes will know their physical status before the training year. This is where cycling, or periodization, plays a critical role in an athlete's progress.

Periodization is a yearly progression in which the training design focuses on specific qualities at specific periods of the year in an effort to reach optimal fitness (power, strength, speed, flexibility, etc.) for a particular event or series of events. The philosophy behind periodization is that training many qualities simultaneously or training without direction will not allow an athlete to optimize any one quality. By choosing blocks of time (weeks, months) to work on specific qualities, at the end of the year or training objective the athlete will have optimized all qualities and should reach peak fitness. Periodization offers the additional advantage of providing a variety of training stimuli through various exercise choices, training intensities, and volumes. The variety helps prevent overtraining and boredom. The periods, or cycles, include mesocycles (monthly) and microcycles (weekly). Macrocycles are yearly blocks of training better suited to younger athletes or athletes who have the luxury of time to prepare for the future. More commonly, mesocycles are used to achieve desired results, and microcycles are the building blocks to those results.

Soccer has four recognized mesocycles—off-season, preseason, in-season, and postseason—which total 52 weeks. The period of optimal soccer fitness should occur during the in-season cycle, the period beginning seven days before the first match and ending the day of the last match, including play-off and championship matches. Off-season is when the soccer athlete develops all the fitness qualities necessary for success. This period includes much work devoted to physical training and relatively little work allocated to soccer training. The length of the preseason varies depending on the length of training camps before the first match of the season. In preseason the emphasis changes from physical training to soccer skills and strategies. Postseason follows the last match of the season and ends on the first day of off-season training.

Rest and recovery is the number-one objective. Although some athletes are not in favor of fully resting during this time, low-intensity exercise is the only acceptable form of activity.

Note that although the emphasis changes during each mesocycle, the importance of each element does not. The emphasis changes only because of the time allotted for the different objectives. Table 1.1 is a general yearly plan for a collegiate soccer team that clearly illustrates how the mesocycles vary in terms of intensity, volume, and emphasis of soccer skills.

Table 1.1   Training periods in a year

	Volume	Intensity	Emphasis
Off-season 28–32 weeks	High-low	Low-high	100% physical
Preseason 2–4 weeks	Med-low	Med-high	75% soccer, 25% physical
In-season 16 weeks	Low	Low-high	90% soccer, 10% physical
Postseason 2–4 weeks	Very low	Very low	90% rest, 10% soccer/physical

By carefully planning each week of training around the in-season peaking objective, periodization produces a map that will give direction to an athlete or team seeking championship physical qualities.

Specificity

As athletes at all levels train, they begin to experiment with different modes and methods. Although fitness training is important, it is essential to understand the training objective.

The number-one objective is to embark on a training regimen that will specifically develop the ultimate soccer athlete. The soccer player must develop a balance of certain physical qualities, so the approach must not be heavily concentrated on any single quality. Remember, the goal is not to become a weightlifter or a 1,500-meter runner but to achieve a graceful combination of these qualities as they apply to soccer. A program specifically designed with the soccer athlete in mind should be clearly different from a program designed for other sports. Specificity of a soccer program will consider which muscles are used, whether anaerobic or aerobic energy sources are important during a match, and how much flexibility is needed to perform at the highest levels. A program that devotes a large amount of time to low-intensity distance running would not be specific to soccer because it would neglect the explosive sprints and short bursts that are a major part of the game. A weight-training program designed to strengthen the legs and make them more powerful would be a soccer-specific program because it would recognize the importance of the lower body in the game.

TRAINING VARIABLES

As explained in the previous section on periodization, it is important to vary the type of training you do throughout the year in order to progress to higher levels of performance. Aside from the type of training, there are a number of other variables, or ingredients, that can be manipulated in a training program.

Volume

Volume is the measure of the quantity of work. Volume is measured by repetitions in weight training, by distance and repetitions in the running program, and by number of responses in a plyometric program.

The effect of using a range of volumes in training is significant. High-volume training programs (low intensity) are usually used to build a base for the athlete. Changes that usually occur are the addition of lean muscle mass through weight training and an improvement in aerobic capacity through cardiovascular work. Low-volume work (medium to high intensity) is associated with an increase in power, speed, absolute strength, and most anaerobic qualities associated with high intensity. Low to moderate intensity with low-volume work is appropriate during a maintenance period or during a modified rest period following high-intensity work. Volume is usually dictated by the accompanying intensity. Typically, the higher the volume, the lower the intensity and vice versa.

Intensity

Intensity is the measure of the quality of training. Intensity, not volume, appears to have the most effect on the body. For the running program, intensity will be determined by the speed of the runs, the distance, and the rest intervals between the runs. An example of a 100 percent intensity sprint is to run the best time possible. Weight-training intensity is the amount of weight lifted per repetition or the average weight lifted for a given exercise, based on the athlete's repetition maximum. If an athlete can squat 200 pounds (91 kilograms), a lift of 100 pounds (45 kilograms) is an intensity of 50 percent. More subjectively, we can also define intensity in weight training as the combination of the weight lifted and the amount of rest between sets. For nonrunning cardiovascular work, intensity is measured by the heart rate during exercise.

Some coaches believe that carrying exercise to muscular failure is the only way to make progress. This is a fallacy. At times the athlete may need to perform an exercise at 80 percent intensity for six repetitions. The same exercise might be performed at 80 percent for one to three repetitions to hasten recovery or increase speed of movement. Each workout will play a significant role in achieving training goals. The alternation from high to low intensity on a weekly and monthly basis is what will bring about the safe and consistent adaptations of speed, strength, power, and endurance. The density of training, defined as an amount of work performed per unit of time, often plays a role in the overall intensity. Shortening the time in which the athlete performs the work can increase the intensity of a given workout. Density and volume give intensity its often-used second definition of severity or difficulty.

Duration

Duration is the length of time it takes to complete a set, workout, or any series of exercise movements. Usually duration applies to the time it takes to finish a workout, whether it be weight training, plyometrics, running, agility drills, skills training, or stretching. Density plays a role in the duration of the training. The duration and the density depend on the intensity and type of training being performed. A workout of long duration must have low intensity, such as light jogging or weightlifting of many repetitions. If a workout is of high intensity, the duration must be short. Sprinting at high speed or performing weightlifting maximums is so fatiguing that the work can only be sustained for a short period.

Frequency

Frequency is how often training occurs. High frequency of training, usually used in the off-season, should bring about greater changes in the body. A lower frequency of training will occur in-season, allowing more time for work on soccer skills and strategies. Again, different modes of training require different frequencies.

Rest and Recovery

The flip side of intensity, volume, duration, and frequency is rest and recovery. In training, more is not better. The athlete walks a fine line between training hard and training too much. The bottom line is that one must "rest to progress." The body rebuilds itself to a higher level of soccer fitness while at rest—during sleep, in light training, or while doing no training at all.

A common by-product of intense training is overtraining. Many overlook the fact that overtraining has both physical and emotional aspects. Lifting, running, jumping, practice sessions, and playing can all contribute to the physical part of overtraining. The thought is that hard, heavy, and often will get the job done. Nothing could be further from the truth. This type of approach will hinder an athlete's soccer development. Emotionally speaking, preparing for matches and training sessions and dealing with the pressure to perform can cause tremendous mental fatigue. When this pressure is combined with the physical aspect, you can bet it will take a toll on performance. Overtraining is not a quantifiable condition. Researchers have tried to diagnose overtraining before it occurs. No single indicator has proved totally effective. Some of the symptoms to be aware of include the following:

- Loss of body weight and loss of appetite
- Excessive muscle tenderness
- Sleep disturbances
- Elevated resting heart rate, elevated blood pressure, or both
- Loss of competitive desire and a lack of enthusiasm for training

It is difficult to distinguish between the symptoms of overtraining and the effects of day-to-day training. Close communication between the coach and athlete as well as thorough monitoring of the training will help eliminate overtraining from any program.

Eliminating overtraining is another desirable outcome of using periodization. Alternating from high-intensity to low-intensity workouts from day to day and week to week can be easily organized when the coach looks at the whole 52-week picture. When the training revolves around being prepared for the competitive season, the coach can tailor the program to avoid excessive training. If a problem arises, the coach and athlete are able to pinpoint exact dates, intensities, volumes, and so on and then modify current and future training. In the end, periodization is the most effective way to prevent overtraining.

TESTING AND EVALUATION

Testing is the only effective and objective way to evaluate a training program. The use of posttesting data permits accurate evaluation of many qualities. A coach will be able to see progress since the athlete's previous tests or compare data with a previous group of players of the same age, position, or experience. The effectiveness of the program can be checked by the amount of progress in the area of emphasis. For instance, if speed was the desired result, a decrease in speed data would indicate that the program design should be addressed, not the athlete. Injury prevention can be assessed through testing by equating an abnormal amount of injuries to an area of weakness, such as hamstring or quadriceps strength and fitness. In a broader scope, coaches can cross-reference many of the scores as checks and balances to validate beliefs. For example, an increase in leg strength can be verified by an increase in vertical-jump scores and speed.

Testing also serves as a motivational tool for the hard-training athlete. When goals are established or a competition of sorts is set up, training and testing intensity seem to rise. When an athlete achieves or surpasses a goal, belief in the program occurs instantly and preparation for future progress begins. Although numerous tests are available, using a limited

battery of tests simplifies the process, making it repeatable and reliable for interpretation and application.

The coach and athlete should work together to set goals. Abundant research in physiology tells us that linear progress through training is impossible. You cannot guarantee a 5 percent increase in physical qualities every test date. If you could, a 100-pound (45-kilogram) squat would become a 265-pound (120-kilogram) squat in 20 eight-week cycles, a little over three years. The same period would change a 500-pound (227-kilogram) squat into a lift of 1,263 pounds (573 kilograms)! Both scenarios are unlikely. The first might not take that long, and the second is impossible. Physical and genetic limitations will make goal setting a trial-and-error proposition. The coach and player should choose goals based on age, sex, training experience, and program emphasis.

You also wouldn't expect to see improvement in technical skills every day. Instead, a player's ball-handling skills will improve in cycles. A player might experience a long period of no apparent progress and then have a dramatic burst of improvement.

The following are some testing guidelines:

1. Follow testing procedures to the letter if you want to accurate test scores to compare with past or future scores.

2. For accurately averaged and standardized results, try to use electronic instruments and the same testing administrators.

3. During testing, update the athletes on current scores—highs, lows, personal records, and so on.

4. Be sure to designate testing dates and times well in advance so that athletes can prepare properly. The schedule should be common knowledge because the training programs will point toward testing periods at the end of training cycles.

5. For accurate interpretation of scores and to prevent injury, athletes who have not dutifully completed the training cycle should not be allowed to test.

6. Players should warm up and perform flexibility exercises before testing.

7. Perform each test no more than five to seven times per year. This frequency of testing allows sufficient training time for goal achievement and lessens the chance for overtraining or injury that might occur with more frequent testing.

Descriptions of the field tests recommended for measuring the athletic abilities of your players are provided below. Be sure to keep accurate records of test scores so progress can be monitored.

60-YARD SPRINT

Objective: To test the first 30 yards (27 meters) for explosive starting ability, the second 30 yards for speed maintenance and mechanics, and the full 60 yards (55 meters) for speed and speed endurance

Procedure: Use timing pieces at 30 yards and 60 yards. After determining the starting stance (upright, four point), timing begins after the athlete's first movement. Record two trials, with two watches per trial, to the nearest 100th of a second and average the times.

NO-STEP VERTICAL JUMP

Objective: To determine vertical power and indications of overall power

Procedure: Measure the athlete for reach with the athlete's feet flat on the ground and one arm extended as far as possible. Mark at the highest point. Starting with the feet in the initial takeoff position, the athlete jumps as high as possible and touches at the apex of the jump. Record the difference between the reach and jump height of three trials to the nearest half inch and record the highest jump. Any movement of the feet before the jump disqualifies that jump.

Two methods are available to record the apex of the jump: (a) chalk the athlete's fingertips and have the athlete mark a wall or overhang with the reach and the jump, or (b) use a Vertec™, which has vanes with premeasured distances that the athlete can touch or knock away.

STANDING LONG JUMP

Objective: To determine horizontal power and indications of overall power

Procedure: Mark off a distance of 6 to 10 feet (1.8 to 3 meters) by half-inch increments. (The distance will be determined by the age and strength of the athletes). The athlete jumps horizontally as far as possible. Measure three jumps to the nearest half inch from the back of the heel closest to the starting line. Record the longest jump. If any movement of the feet occurs before the jump or if the athlete falls backward after landing, the jump is disqualified.

300-YARD SHUTTLE

Objective: To determine anaerobic endurance

Procedure: Mark off 50 yards (46 meters) with testers at 0 yards and 50 yards. The first move starts the clock. The athlete runs 50 yards and touches the marked line with one foot, turns around, and runs back, completing three round trips. If the athlete fails to touch or pass a line, the time is disqualified. Record the time to the nearest 100th of a second.

BENCH PRESS

Objective: To determine upper-body strength (that is, the strength of chest, shoulders, triceps, and pressing stabilizers)

Procedure: With spotters on each side of the weightlifting bar, the athlete begins with the bar at arm's length. The athlete lowers the bar and after touching (no bouncing) the chest, immediately lifts the bar to the starting position. Bouncing or heaving the bar from the chest, raising the buttocks from the bench, or failing to produce upward movement during the pressing phase disqualifies the test. Permit no more than three attempts at a given weight and allow attempts at no more than three weights. (For a more in-depth instruction for the bench press, see page 76.)

SQUAT OR LEG PRESS

Objective: To determine lower-body strength (that is, the strength of thighs, lower back, and torso)

Procedure: With spotters on each side of the bar or press, the athlete lowers the weight to a predetermined knee-joint angle (90 degrees is commonly used but that angle can be modified for individual preference). The lift is complete when the athlete returns to the starting position. Improper form or incomplete knee-joint angle is cause for termination or disqualification of the lift. Permit no more than three attempts at a given weight and allow attempts at no more than three weights. (The squat can be found on page 71 and the leg press on page 70.)

CLEAN PULL

Objective: To determine total body power

Procedure: Begin by determining how high the bar must be lifted for a successful attempt (for example, two-thirds of the lifter's height or the height of the shoulders). The lower the height selected, the less involved the total body is in performing the lift and the greater the injury risk is to the lower back because of the heavier weight. From the starting position the lifter begins the lift and finishes when the bar is back on the floor. Permit no more than three attempts at a given weight and allow attempts at no more than three weights. (The clean pull exercise can be found on page 74.)

EVALUATING TEST SCORES

Physical testing is used for three essential reasons: for gathering information, for comparing the data, and for determining training procedures based on the results of the testing. Initial results of an athlete's skill tests are called the baseline scores. Evaluators can use these scores to compare one athlete's results to other athletes' results, or an athlete's results can be compared to the same athlete's data gathered at a later date. Evaluators can then make necessary adjustments to training regimens.

Soccer players generally range in age from 6 to 30, and the variety of skill levels within this age range has a great influence on physical testing data. Thus it would be too lengthy to list physical testing scores for all categories. However, in the case of the many age and skill-level categories for soccer, it would be misleading to follow guidelines that do not pertain to an athlete's particular situation. That is why comparing an athlete's test scores to the previous baseline test scores is a better way to evaluate a training program and its effects on each player. Even though the numbers for each athlete are different, the correct rate of progress can still be measured by the percentage of improvements made by other players or the percentage of increase in team averages.

Comparison means assessing similarities and differences between one vertical jump and another vertical jump, one leg press and another leg press, and so on. Evaluation is the interpretation of the comparisons. Finding that athlete A's bench press result is lower than the results of other players at that position or lower than the team average is an example of evaluation. Or, finding that athlete B's leg press is statistically excellent, but speed and vertical jump tests are below average, is another example. The final step is using the evaluation to determine training modifications for a more beneficial outcome before the next testing period.

Let's go through an example of the full process:

	Leg press	No-step vertical jump	60-yd sprint
Athlete A	500 lbs (227 kg)	22" (56 cm)	8.00 sec
Team average	350 lbs (159 kg)	27" (69 cm)	7.40 sec

Comparison: Athlete A's leg press is 150 lbs (68 kilograms) higher than the team average, A's no-step vertical jump is 5 inches (13 centimeters) lower, and A's 60-yard (55-meter) sprint is .60 second slower.

Evaluation: The leg strength is excellent but the power tests are low compared to leg strength. With a leg press that strong, there is an indication that the power tests should be better than the team average.

Determination: There is a need to focus on plyometric training to improve the jumping and sprinting numbers as well as a need to reevaluate Athlete A's running technique and conditioning. The leg press program should remain the same with a slight reduction in volume if necessary. This will reduce the possibility of fatigue so that Athlete A is fresh for plyometric drills and is likely to improve his speed.

CHAPTER 2

FLEXIBILITY AND WARM-UP

The importance of being flexible

and warming up properly cannot be overstated. For optimal training and match performance, players should stretch and warm up every time before activity.

Although warming up and stretching are performed in tandem, they have different objectives and results. Players must never confuse the two activities. Flexibility exercises are used to increase the length of the muscles and increase the range of motion about a joint. Warm-up, the movement link between stretching and the game, progressively prepares the athlete for competition. Let us look at the definitions of both.

WARM-UP

An effective warm-up includes gamelike movement that prepares the athlete for all-out effort. An athlete should perform multidirectional movements that slowly but progressively increase toward 100 percent effort. The warm-up should begin with slow, simple movements and move toward quicker, more complex gamelike movements.

Injury is often related to a lack of pretraining and precompetition warm-up. On the other hand, some athletes with poor flexibility are injury free. Hamstrings of even the most flexible athletes are not immune to muscle pulls. The warm-up serves three valuable purposes. First, it raises body temperature in a progressive manner, enabling the muscles to contract and relax more easily, thus making movement more effective. Second, it increases blood flow, making more oxygen and nutrients available to working muscles. Third, if it is soccer related it can provide a practice effect and enhance players' skills through repetition.

If players do not perform a proper soccer-related warm-up that progressively increases body temperature, the possibility of injury increases and performance will likely decrease.

FLEXIBILITY

Gained through passive (assisted) or active (self-administered) effort, flexibility is acquired predominantly by stretching. Increasing range of motion at a joint by increasing the length of the muscle or muscles associated with the joint is the primary objective. With good flexibility, players can perform soccer movements like shooting, feinting, and attacking with correct technique and less risk of injury. For example, an inflexible lower body makes it difficult to run at top speed, strike the ball properly, or get good height in the air while jumping. As far as injury is concerned, the most dangerous positions occur when the body is unexpectedly subjected to extreme ranges of motion. Losing one's footing or being tripped and falling into an awkward position are typical examples. If an athlete has better-than-average range of motion, these positions are less likely to be risky.

The two basic types of stretching are static stretching and ballistic stretching. Static stretching generally means a slow stretching effort in which the athlete reaches a point of a light burning or an inability to stretch any farther. The athlete then holds the position for a given time, ranging from 5 to 30 seconds or more. The athlete can repeat the stretch two or three times. In ballistic stretching the athlete performs the same stretching steps but instead of holding the stretch, he or she repeatedly recoils and stretches the muscle in a bouncing manner.

Bouncing, or ballistic stretching, is appropriately denounced because the practice increases the risk of injury. When a muscle is rapidly and forcibly stretched, special mechanisms in the muscle bring about an immediate contraction. This circumstance can cause pulls or strains. Although static stretching is safe and effective, we prefer what is termed

the *ballistic controlled* method. Instead of holding a position for a given period, the athlete continually reaches or pushes the stretch in a deliberate, controlled manner. When the athlete feels a light burning sensation or progress has stopped, he or she relaxes and immediately resumes the stretch. The player should push the stretch for 5 to 10 seconds and repeat three or four times. More aggressive than the basic static method, a ballistic controlled stretch activates the muscles and nervous system in a more vigorous fashion and does not take as long as the basic method.

SEQUENCE OF PREPARATION FOR TRAINING OR COMPETITION

Players must perform the stretching routine and warm-up in the proper order. Although various routines may be equally effective, we feel that the following sequencing best suits the soccer athlete: light movement or easy jogging; joint movement; stretching sequences with the standing upper body, the standing lower body, and the seated and lying lower body; and finally the warm-up.

Step 1: Light Movement

Light movement, juggling, or a short-distance jog starts the body in motion and starts the blood flowing to the musculature while creating an avenue for the increase in body temperature to come. The jog can be between 400 and 1,200 yards (366 to 1097 meters) and the low-intensity movement drills (backpedaling, jogging, lateral shuffles, etc.) can be repeated over a distance of 10 to 20 yards (9 to 18 meters).

Step 2: Joint Movement

Working from the inside out, the athlete starts by loosening the joints, tendons, and ligaments. Moving the joints back and forth or in a circular motion will help lubricate the joints and serve as the beginning of dynamic movement.

BIG ARM CIRCLES

Focus: Shoulders

Procedure: With your arms outstretched laterally and straight, make three- to four-foot circles by rotating at the shoulder.

Duration: 15 to 20 circles, then change direction

Variation: Alternate hand position, palm up or palm down.

SMALL ARM CIRCLES

Focus: Shoulders

Procedure: With your arms outstretched laterally and straight, make 6- to 12-inch (15- to 30-centimeter) circles by rotating at the shoulder.

Duration: 30 to 40 circles, then change direction

Variation: Alternate hand position, palm up or palm down.

STANDING TWIST

Focus: Lower back and trunk

Procedure: With your arms outstretched laterally, twist at the waist with minimal turning of your hips. Maintain your feet in the starting position. The turn should be smooth and take about one second.

Duration: 15 to 30 seconds

TWIST BEHIND

Focus: Lower back and trunk

Procedure: Follow the same procedure you used for the standing twist, but perform a full turn to face the direction opposite that of the stance. The turning of your hip is necessary. Do one turn every two seconds.

Duration: 15 to 30 seconds

Variation: Without turning your hips, twist as fast as you can. Your head should be fixed straight ahead, and the twist should bring your shoulder to your chin.

HIP FLEXOR ROTATION

Focus: Lower back, lower abdominals, hip flexors

Procedure: Place your hands on your hips, set your feet at shoulder-width, and bend your knees slightly. Rotate your upper body clockwise at your waist in the biggest circle possible.

Duration: 10 to 15 circles in one direction, then change direction

Variation: Perform the exercise with your legs straight. A second variation is to stretch your arms overhead through the entire movement to stretch your rib cage.

KNEE FLEX

Focus: Knee joint

Procedure: Stand with your feet close together and place your hands on your knees. Continually flex your knees, no farther than about 30 degrees.

Duration: 20 to 30 repetitions

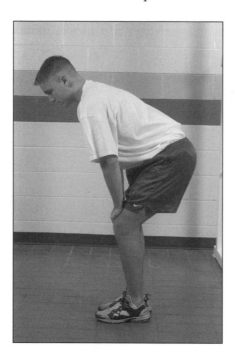 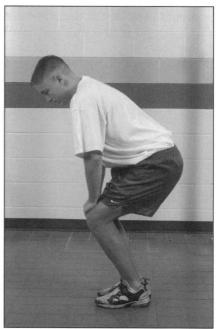

KNEE CIRCLES

Focus: Knee joint

Procedure: Using the same starting position you used for the knee flex, rotate your knees in a clockwise or counterclockwise movement.

Duration: 10 to 15 repetitions in each direction

HEEL AND TOE RAISE

Focus: Gastrocnemius, soleus, and tibialis anterior

Procedure: With your legs straight, rock up on your toes while flexing your calf and then rock back on your heels with your toes pointing up.

Duration: 15 to 20 repetitions for each movement

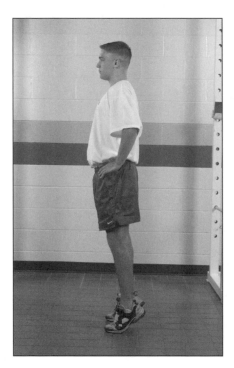 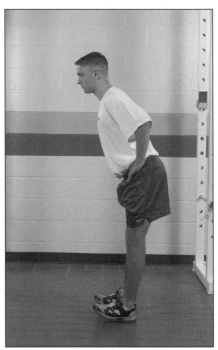

Step 3: Standing Upper-Body Stretches

Following the loosening of the joints, athletes should perform upper-body stretches in a standing position, using the ballistic controlled method described earlier. The sequence begins with the neck and arms, then moves to the upper back, chest, rib cage, and lower trunk. Stretches should include twisting and lateral bending of the trunk.

LATERAL REACH

Focus: Shoulders, upper and lower back

Procedure: Set your feet wider than shoulder-width. Put your right hand on your right hip. Turn to the right and reach across with your left arm extended. Foot movement should be minimal. Repeat to the other side.

Duration: Continuous reach, not hold, 15 to 20 seconds to each side

Variation: Reach up or down across your body at a 45-degree angle. Your hand position will change shoulder emphasis.

OVERHEAD LATERAL BEND

Focus: Rib cage, obliques, triceps, latissimus dorsi

Procedure: Set your feet at hip-width. Put your right hand on your right hip and extend your left arm straight up. Bend and reach to the right side and repeat to the left.

Duration: Continuous reach, not hold, 15 to 20 seconds to each side

Variation: Extend both arms overhead. A slight bend at the knees will change the focus of the lower back and obliques.

TRICEPS AND LATISSIMUS STRETCH

Focus: Triceps, latissimus dorsi, rib cage

Procedure: Hold your right elbow with your left hand behind your head. Bend laterally to the left. Repeat to the right.

Duration: Continuous stretch, not hold, for 15 to 20 seconds

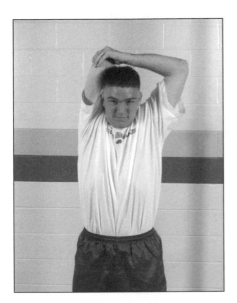 

POSTERIOR SHOULDER STRETCH

Focus: Posterior shoulder and upper back

Procedure: Hold your left elbow with your right hand in front and close to your chest. Squeeze and pull. Repeat with your right arm.

Duration: Continuous stretch, not hold, for 15 to 20 seconds

Variation: While stretching your left shoulder, turn your trunk as far as possible to the right.

Step 4: Standing Lower-Body Stretches

Standing lower-body stretches begin the lower-body work. Step 4 helps to loosen the lower back, gluteus maximus, and hamstrings. Athletes can more effectively stretch these muscles when standing than when seated.

STANDING HAMSTRING

Focus: Lower back, gluteus, hamstrings, and calves

Procedure: Spread your legs about twice the width of your shoulders. Keeping your legs straight and your head in line with your upper body, reach with both arms to your right foot, to the middle of the stance, and to your left foot. Bend both knees before rising and moving to stretch the next area.

Duration: Continuous stretch, not hold, for 15 to 20 seconds in each position

Variation: One way to maintain a continuous stretch is to set a progression. For example, with both hands reach first to your knee, then your calf, then your ankle, and finally to the top of your foot. You can increase the intensity of the calf stretch by keeping your toe off the floor while stretching.

LATERAL GROIN STRETCH

Focus: Groin, hamstrings

Procedure: Squat over your right leg with your heel flat or on your toes. Facing forward, extend your left leg laterally, resting your foot on your heel. The focus of the stretch will change with the lean of your upper body (forward or left) and the direction in which you point your foot (straight up or forward).

Duration: 15 to 20 seconds in each direction

THREE-POINT LUNGE

Focus: Gluteus, hamstrings, hip flexors

Procedure: Start in the lunge position—left knee on the floor with your lower leg behind your body and right leg in front of your body with the foot flat on the floor and your knee at 90 degrees. For position 1, maintain your upper body in an upright position while pushing forward. For position 2, turn to the left and lower your right elbow toward the floor inside your right leg. For position 3, grab your left foot with your right hand. Pull it to your buttocks and lean forward.

Duration: 15 to 20 seconds at each position

Step 5: Seated and Lying Lower-Body Stretches

The final step of stretching comprises the lower-body stretches, which are performed seated and lying and include some twisting and lateral bending of the trunk.

SEATED HAMSTRING

Focus: Lower back, hamstrings, and calves

Procedure: Sit and spread your legs as far as is comfortable. With your arms outstretched, reach toward your left foot, toward your right foot, and then forward, keeping your head and chest up.

Duration: Continuous stretch, not hold, for 15 to 20 seconds in each position

Variation: Reach with your left hand to your right foot to include some oblique activity and increase the hamstring stretch.

BUTTERFLY

Focus: Groin

Procedure: In a seated position bring both feet into the middle of your body as far as is comfortable. Hold both feet with both hands and pull your chest to your feet.

Duration: Continuous stretch, not hold, for 15 to 20 seconds

Variation: Place feet farther from your body and reach to the floor in front.

I-T BAND STRETCH

Focus: Iliotibial band, gluteus

Procedure: From the butterfly position, maintain the position of your right leg but place your left leg behind your body. Attempt to place your chest on top of your right knee. Repeat the procedure to your left knee.

Duration: 15 to 20 seconds

Variation: Raise your body off the floor and over your front leg.

LYING LOWER BACK

Focus: Lower back

Procedure: Lying on your back with your arms outstretched to the side of your body at 90 degrees, raise your left leg to a position perpendicular to the floor and then lower it to your right hand. It is not necessary to keep your leg straight when lowering it to your hand.

Duration: 15 to 20 seconds

Variation: After raising your leg, hold it behind your calf and pull toward your body for 10 to 15 seconds before lowering your leg to your hand.

Step 6: Warm-Up

The warm-up begins immediately following the last stretch. The player has stretched her entire body, and now the warm-up, with and without the ball, can begin. The player should observe several guidelines in warming up:

1. Begin with the simplest, slowest movements.
2. Progressively build intensity, complexity, and speed.
3. A repetition distance of 20 to 30 yards (18 to 27 meters) is sufficient.
4. Use forward, backward, lateral, and angular movements.
5. Use upper-body movements (arm swings, etc.) in concert with your lower body.
6. Include hops, skips, and jumps with one or both legs.
7. Change speed, direction, or both in a running segment of 20 to 30 yards (18 to 27 meters).
8. The warm-up session should last as long as it takes to raise your body temperature adequately. Break a good sweat and without hesitation perform activity at 100 percent intensity, including sprinting, jumping, and striking.

Although various routines are feasible, notice the progression of the following menu. It gradually increases the activity level of the athlete, eventually combining drills. Players should perform at least two repetitions of each drill.

HIGH KNEES

Focus: Arm carry and body lean for proper running technique and preparation of the hip flexors and lower leg for activity

Procedure:

- Keep your upper body in an upright position.
- Arm action should be identical to the action you use when running.
- While moving forward, rapidly lift your knees to waist height.
- Keep your feet underneath your body. Do not extend your foot forward.

BUTT KICKS

Focus: Hamstring and lower leg

Procedure:

- Keep your upper body in an upright position.
- Arm action should be identical to the action you use when running.
- While moving forward, rapidly lift your heels to your gluteus.
- Try to keep your upper legs in line with your upright body.

BACKWARD RUN

Focus: Gluteus, hamstring, and lower leg as well as arm-carry technique and body lean

Procedure:

- Body lean should be forward.
- Arm action should be identical to the action you use when running forward.
- Lift your foot to your buttocks and kick it straight back and down to the ground.
- Arm action is critical for the correct extension of your legs backward.

SHUFFLE

Focus: Abductors and adductors of the thigh

Procedure:

- Move laterally in a heel-to-heel fashion.
- Speed is not important.
- Your arms should be relaxed at 90 degrees to the side of your body.

SHUFFLE FOR SPEED

Focus: Abductors and adductors of the thigh

Procedure:

- To ensure speed, hold your center of gravity much lower than you do in the regular shuffle.
- Your feet should never come together. Maintain a wide base.
- Arm activity should be aggressive and should contribute to balance.
- Move as fast as possible.

TWO-LEGGED HOPS

Focus: Preparation of the body and legs for dynamic activity

Procedure:

- Keep your feet together.
- Use your arms aggressively and repetitively.
- Jump as far and as high as possible while maintaining balance. Maintaining balance after the landing will demonstrate correct technique.
- Landing and takeoff should be rapid.

ONE-LEGGED HOPS FOR DISTANCE

Focus: Progression from the two-legged hop

Procedure:

- Arm carry and action should be similar to the action you use when running.
- Hop for distance while maintaining balance.
- Your body should lean forward slightly.
- Speed is not important.

ONE-LEGGED HOPS FOR SPEED

Focus: Progression from one-legged hops for distance with movement as fast as possible

Procedure:

- The action is similar to the action you would use to sprint on one leg.
- Arm action is aggressive.
- Your body lean will be slight, but your center of gravity will be lower.
- Hops should be short and as fast as balance and technique will allow.

BACKPEDAL SLOW AND FAST

Focus: Body lean for balance and change of speed

Procedure:

- Divide your warm-up distance into two equal lengths.
- Backpedal the first section smoothly with your body somewhat upright.
- Backpedal the second section as fast as technique will allow. Lower your center of gravity.

SHUFFLE SLOW AND FAST

Focus: Body lean for balance and change of speed

Procedure:

- Divide your warm-up distance into two equal lengths.
- Perform the first section with a slow heel-to-heel movement.
- Do the second section as fast as technique will allow. Lower your center of gravity.

JOG AND STRIDE

Focus: Change of speed

Procedure:

- Divide your warm-up distance into two equal lengths.
- Slowly jog the first section.
- Aggressively change speed and stride for the second section.

STRIDE AND SPRINT

Focus: Change of speed

Procedure:

- Divide your warm-up distance into two equal lengths.
- Stride the first section.
- Sprint the second section.

SHUFFLE AND SPRINT

Focus: Change of speed, direction, and body position

Procedure:

- Divide your warm-up distance into two equal lengths.
- Shuffle the first section at medium to full speed.
- For the second section, aggressively turn and sprint.

SPRINT AND BACKPEDAL

Focus: Change of speed, direction, and body position

Procedure:

- Sprint the entire designated distance, usually half of the warm-up distance.
- At the end of the distance rapidly change direction into a backpedal.

CHAPTER 3

STRENGTH TRAINING

Strength is the ability of a muscle

to overcome resistance or the ability to resist force. The strength of the muscular contraction determines how strong the athlete is.

If finesse and speed are the tools of superstar soccer athletes, strength training is the most effective way to attain championship soccer. Here is a look at how strength affects certain physical qualities:

• **Strength and speed.** A soccer player must be strong to withstand the training that it takes to increase speed. Because training for speed is dynamic and aggressive, an athlete who lacks strength is subject to the risk of serious injury.

• **Strength and vertical jump.** Athletes who jump high for headers or keeper saves have one thing in common: they have above-average leg strength. If players want to jump high or increase their vertical jump, becoming stronger is the first step.

• **Strength and endurance.** When players' legs become heavy from running far and fast during a match, the strength of their legs carries them that "extra mile." Soccer games are often won or lost in the last five minutes of each half. Endurance can make the difference between winning and losing.

• **Strength and agility.** A player who changes direction by cutting left and then right would appear to be in slow motion if he lacked the strength to plant his foot and aggressively drive his body in the desired direction. Athletes who make quick and decisive movements have the strength to weave their way up field for the score.

• **Strength and durability.** Make no mistake about it; the stronger athlete becomes injured less often and less severely. Durability is directly linked to the body's ability to withstand stress. Strength gives the body that ability.

• **Strength and upper-body soccer.** Any player who has been caught in a group of opposing players in a contest for the ball knows how important upper-body strength is. Although soccer is a lower-body-dominated sport, players must not neglect upper-body strength. Upper-body strength is necessary for the complete soccer player.

DESIGNING A PROGRAM

This chapter includes some sample strength-training programs. The generality of these workouts, however, may not address the specific needs of every athlete. Therefore, we will discuss the steps involved in designing a program from the beginning so that the coach or soccer athlete can better tailor a program to individual needs.

1. **Determine the physiology of soccer.** What energy sources are involved? Of the energy sources involved, what percentage of the game is dedicated to those sources? The training program should be designed based on the demands of the game and the needs of the athlete, which will be determined by the style of play or the team philosophy. As an example, a midfielder who relies on speed and a physical style of play should devote the majority of her program to training for power and absolute strength. The team that builds from the back using a slower paced game plan should spend less time on speed and sprint training and more time on longer distance interval training.

2. **What are the major biomechanics of soccer?** Analysis of the demands of the game and the needs of the athlete shows that the

majority of the movement in soccer involves the lower body. The bulk of the menu and the training emphasis should be on the lower body rather than the chest and shoulders.

3. **Consider administrative liabilities.** Managerial concerns include everything from who gets the weight-room key to how much time is available. Probably the biggest hurdles will be supervision, facility, and time. How many times will training occur per week? For how many weeks in a year? For how many minutes in a day? How many qualified supervisors are required for each group? How many athletes can safely fit into the facility? These programming variables must be considered when laying out the strength-training program.

4. **Evaluate your facility.** Many equipment manufacturers in the United States make complicated and effective machines for strengthening. Not every gym is outfitted with state-of-the-art equipment or even full lines of equipment. After determining the training menu, the next decision involves evaluating your equipment. Will the equipment be effective for achieving the goals of the program design? Is the equipment safe for training both small and large groups? How much supervision will be needed for the specific size of the facility?

5. **Assess coaching skills.** You must objectively evaluate whether you can coach the techniques and philosophies. Information in books or from other coaches can be extremely helpful. Many times, however, coaches learn about the latest approaches and try to apply them without having the experience or skills to convey the information properly to athletes. As a result, the program comes up short of the desired goal or results in injury. The message here is that you should teach only what you know and stick to the basics when in doubt.

MISCONCEPTIONS ABOUT STRENGTH TRAINING

Many misconceptions exist about strength training. Some of the most frequently expressed concerns include the following.

Soccer players will lose flexibility if they intensely strength train. Strength training does not hinder any athlete. Incorrect strength training does. This statement should generally blanket any questions concerning ill effects of strength training for soccer athletes. Specifically, when a periodized strength program with a clear objective is implemented, this means that all other physically related variables (conditioning, flexibility, matches, travel, etc.) are considered. Therefore, performing the correct exercises with a full range of motion should not only increase strength but also increase flexibility. For example, an exercise such as a one-legged squat can stretch the hamstrings and glutes and at the same time begin to develop strength in a greater range of motion.

Strength training will make players too bulky to play the game. Before a strength program is designed it is necessary to define the objective. The goal may be to increase speed, build lean muscle mass, or increase absolute strength. *Bulk* is a term that is associated with an excessive increase in muscle mass and body weight and a decrease in flexibility. There may be good reasons for adding lean muscle mass—to increase durability, to add size to create a more physical defender, to be part of a long-term plan to develop more power. When planned correctly, strength training will be an asset to a well-developed soccer athlete and will not hinder performance. Proper design should cause no excessive weight gain. Additional lean body weight will only enhance an athlete's performance.

Finally, you must remember that strength training is only one component of a conditioning program. A negative effect will result only from negligent planning.

Strength training will slow players down. Let us answer this question in a backward fashion. It is difficult for an athlete to obtain optimal speed *without* strength training. Except for track and field athletes, most athletes have poor running mechanics to a certain degree, which adversely affects running speed. Although correcting running flaws will certainly increase speed, strength training is the only way to produce the power needed to increase speed dramatically. The appropriate design is important. An athlete cannot possibly become slower when performing the right program. If there is any question that weight training will slow down an athlete, you need only look at the physiques of the world's fastest sprinters.

Strength training is unsafe. Training of any type involves some risk. However, risk can be greatly diminished if athletes observe several precautionary measures:

1. Always use a spotter.
2. Never train alone.
3. Always check for correct poundage.
4. Wear properly fitted clothes and footwear.
5. Call attention to uncommon aches, pains, and illnesses.
6. Consult a physician before starting a program.
7. Always perform a proper flexibility and warm-up program before training (see chapter 2).
8. Never sacrifice form for poundage. Always use correct technique.

Strength training will make better soccer players. Directly, no! Indirectly, without question. Great athletes possess many positive attributes. We can control many variables, such as determination, work ethic, and preparation. We cannot control other things, such as our genetic limits for speed and strength. The point is that getting big and strong is not the only thing that will ensure success. What strength training will do is

1. decrease the risk and severity of injury;
2. increase durability;
3. increase speed, power, and strength—the tools for success; and
4. give the athlete one more way to become a great player.

SELECTION OF EQUIPMENT

Many training facilities contain various pieces of training equipment that do not come from the same manufacturer. It can be a little intimidating to walk into a weight room and see so many different pieces of exercise equipment. Typically, it comes down to two basic modes of training—free weights and machines.

Machines

Machines offer the ability to isolate a specific muscle group without involving stabilizing musculature surrounding the area. The range of motion and adjustable weight stacks make the units safe and easy to operate. Unfortunately, the safety factor and the isolation feature come in exchange for some important developmental factors. Isolating specific muscles is a function of track resistance (restricted movement in one direction), which in turn does not require any balance or coordination of movement. Balance and coordination are key factors in the soccer world, and players must do anything they can to improve in those areas.

Soccer, like most sports, is a multiple-joint-movement activity. Machines cannot duplicate the movement of more than one joint at a time. Again, for a more beneficial carryover (specificity) to soccer, players should perform exercises that involve more than one muscle group. An athlete does not move by the working of individual muscles. All muscle groups work together to perform movement.

Lagging body parts or rehabilitation efforts, however, can benefit greatly from the use of certain machines. Beginning athletes or athletes with a poor strength base would also see positive results from using particular exercise machines at different times of the year.

Among the types of machines are plate-loaded machines, pneumatic (air-powered) machines, and pulley-cable systems. Cable systems are not completely track resistant and thus offer a little more freedom of movement. This type of machine is a necessity for some exercises.

Free Weights

Fundamentally, free-weight training offers a more complete training effect. Balance, coordination, and accommodation of body types are some of the basic training responses that occur with free-weight training. Scientific research points to other benefits that cannot be achieved by machines, ideas that are better addressed in another book.

An athlete must teach her body to adjust to different environments on the field. A machine has a given dimension and movement pattern that cannot be altered, but a barbell or dumbbell will completely accommodate an athlete of any size.

Because of the need to coordinate free-weight movements, the lifter must use stabilizing muscles. Think of the muscles involved in a back squat other than the quadriceps and gluteus maximus. Abdominal, soleus, lower back, and hamstrings are not primary movers, but they provide balance and assistance just as they do in running.

Although both training modes have pluses and minuses, a complete weight-training program should include a mixture of free weights and machines.

TERMINOLOGY

To understand philosophies and objectives, you must be familiar with certain strength-training terms. The following list should eliminate confusion about the correct definitions, which are often interchanged or misinterpreted.

cheating—Using extra motion from other parts of the body to complete a movement. For example, leaning back and swinging the arms to finish a biceps curl is an advanced technique for bodybuilders that has little use in the training of soccer athletes. Cheating can increase the risk of injury because adding momentum to a weight can load the muscle above its capacity.

forced repetitions—Receiving assistance from a spotter to finish a movement while maintaining strict form. This method is usually used to perform more repetitions after complete fatigue. This advanced weight-training technique might be used to fatigue the muscle further, but it should not be used if the lifting athlete can no longer control the bar.

hypertrophy—In scientific terms, hypertrophy means growth. Hypertrophy is caused by varying degrees of stress, but it is usually a result of weight training in general. The repetition zone that seems to be most productive for gaining size is between 6 and 12. This repetition zone is also good for developing a base leading into strength-training phases that have lower repetition ranges.

power—Probably the most used but least understood term in the training of athletes, the term *power* is written as force + distance ÷ time. Power, unlike strength, is entirely dependent on time. Power is demonstrated by creating the most force in the least amount of time. The longer a movement takes, the less powerful it is. Thus, another term for power is *speed-strength*. A good point to remember is that the heaviest weight moved does not always create the most power unless speed is a factor.

strict form—Perfect technique when performing exercises, with no extra momentum or inertia thrown into the movement to finish the exercise. Strict form is the preferred technique because it is the best way to evaluate strength from repetition to repetition.

full range of motion—Each exercise has a beginning position and finishing position. The athlete must use the full range of exercise motion to gain the benefits of an exercise. By not using the full motion the athlete may be able to use more weight or find it easier to reach the finished position. But failing to perform the exercise correctly will limit strength gains and decrease the flexibility of the muscle and joint. More likely, the athlete will become injured during the exercise or later in practice or a match because of poor conditioning.

PROGRAMS

Literally dozens of combinations of objectives and lifting schedules have been proposed. We will provide some basic programming samples that a coach can implement or use to stimulate thought about how to create other programs for specific situations.

Two-Day Training

Training twice per week is the minimum frequency for a total program and the fewest number of training days that can produce a training effect.

Strengths

- Two days of training allows time for work on other qualities, such as speed and conditioning.
- Good for beginning athletes.
- Good in-season format.

Weaknesses

- Minimum requirement for results.
- Unable to emphasize a body part.
- Limited menu.

Design Tips

- Schedule 48 hours between workouts.
- Limit training time to keep intensity high.

Sample I.

Monday
Clean pull

Back squat

Hyperextension

Leg curl

Bench press

Thursday
Military press

Lat pulldown

Triceps pushdown

Barbell curl

Sample II.

Monday
Bench press

Incline press

Barbell shrug

Dumbbell lateral raise

Lying triceps extension

Wednesday
Leg press

Hyperextension

Leg curl

Seated calf raise

Barbell curl

Three-Day Training

Training three times per week is a common design that allows for enough menu expansion and rest between workouts to permit good progress.

Strengths
- Preferable in-season design.
- Offers abundant rest between workouts.
- Good length of menu for variety.

Weaknesses
- Some exercises receive only 48 hours of rest between bouts.
- The program might work the upper and lower body all three days.

Design Tips
- Try to keep length of training time equal for all three days.
- Keep in mind conditioning and other components when planning heavy weight-training days.

Sample I.

Monday	Wednesday	Friday
Bench press	Bench press	Dumbbell lateral raise
Incline dumbbell press	Incline dumbbell press	Front alternate raise
Dumbbell lateral raise	Seated row	Seated row
Front alternate raise	Lat pulldown	Lat pulldown
Lying triceps extension	Lying triceps extension	Dumbbell curls
Dumbbell curls	Leg press	Leg press
	Lunges	Lunges
	Leg curls	Leg curls

Sample II.

Monday	Wednesday	Friday
Dumbbell bench press	Lat pulldown	Squat
Incline press	Dumbbell row	Hyperextension
Military press	Barbell curl	Leg curl
Bent lateral raise	Triceps pushdown	Standing calf
Shrug		

Four-Day Training

Training four days per week usually uses a split, which finds one workout for Monday and Thursday and the other on Tuesday and Friday.

Strengths

- This format divides workouts into two separate days—upper body—lower body, pushing-pulling, power-strength.
- Allows 72 hours between workouts, an interval better suited for muscular growth and strength gains.
- Favorable off-season design. Difficult but not impossible in-season.

Weakness

- Permits only one complete day off.

Design Tips

- When lifting heavy, it might be necessary to lighten the second half of the week by up to 20 percent.
- Schedule conditioning around leg work.
- Try to use the off day for total rest.

Sample I.

Monday and Thursday
Dumbbell bench press

Dumbbell incline press

Dumbbell lateral raise

Dumbbell shrug

Triceps pushdown

Tuesday and Friday
Lat pulldown

Seated row

Barbell curl

Leg extension

Back squat

Leg curl

Sample II.

Monday and Thursday
Incline press

Military press

Lat pulldown

Seated row

Barbell curl

Lying triceps extension

Tuesday and Friday
Clean pull

Leg press

Leg extension

Leg curl

Hyperextension

Seated calf

Sample III.

Monday
Clean pull

Clean deadlift

Standing calf raise

Seated calf raise

Tuesday
Dumbbell bench press

Military press

Bent lateral raise

Lying triceps extension

Thursday

Lat pulldown

Dumbbell row

Alternate dumbbell curl

Friday

Squat

Lunge

Leg curl

Hypertrophy and Strength

The hypertrophy and strength format is ideal for athletes who have above-average strength in a particular area but lack the size or foundation to develop strength in other areas.

Strengths

- Can be built into any program.
- Can target any area for specific development.
- Will help the athlete maintain optimal weight while gaining strength.

Weakness

- Appropriate only for intermediate to advanced athletes.

Design Tips

- Make sure that the athlete is fully developed before becoming too specific.
- Assign specific percentages or weights to strength exercises.

For example, let us assume that an athlete has good upper-body strength but needs more size in the lower body to train for strength in the future.

Monday and Thursday (strength)

Incline press 5 × 3

Triceps pushdown 5 × 5

Military press 3 × 3

Seated row 5 × 5

Dumbbell row 5 × 5

Alternate dumbbell curl 3 × 5

Tuesday and Friday (hypertrophy)

Leg extension 3 × 30

Leg press 5 × 12

Lunge 3 × 12

Clean deadlift 3 × 12

Leg curls 5 × 12

Standing calf raise 3 × 20

Five-Day Emphasis

The five-day program is an excellent off-season approach for all objectives—strength, size, power, or a more focused intensity. Days 1, 3, and 5 are used for the emphasis, and days 2 and 4 are for the remainder of the training menu.

Strengths

- Workouts can be split into upper body and lower body, or the three emphasis days can focus on a particular body part.
- The program offers the opportunity to raise intensity because the emphasis is spread over three days rather than one or two.
- Workouts can target any lagging body part or physical quality.

Weaknesses

- Appropriate for off-season format only.
- Permits no off days during the training week, which means that conditioning will always be on a weight-training day.
- The format could lead to overtraining or fatigue, so it should be used only for advanced athletes.

Design Tips

- Do not deemphasize days 2 and 4; these days are a valuable part of the training.
- If the emphasis is on the lower body, be alert for fatigue in the lower back.

Emphasis: Lower-body hypertrophy

Monday, Wednesday, Friday

Leg extension 20–30 reps

Back squat 8–12 reps

Lunge 8–12 reps

Clean deadlift 6–10 reps

Hyperextension 12–15 reps

Leg curl 8–12 reps

Tuesday and Thursday
Bench press 3–5 reps

Dumbbell shrug 5 reps

Dumbbell lateral raise 5 reps

Dumbbell row 5 reps

Lat pulldown 5 reps

Lying triceps extension 5–8 reps

Alternate dumbbell curl 5–8 reps

Emphasis: Lower-body strength

Monday
Clean pull 3–5 reps

Clean deadlift 3–5 reps

Leg curl 5–8 reps

Friday
Clean pull 3–5 reps

Leg press 3–5 reps

Seated calf raise 12–15 reps

Wednesday
Leg press 3–5 reps

Clean deadlift 3–5 reps

Seated calf 12–15 reps

Leg curl 5–8 reps

Tuesday and Thursday
Incline press 3–5 reps

Seated row 5–8 reps

Dumbbell lateral raise 5–8 reps

Shrug 5–8 reps

Lying triceps extension 5–8 reps

Barbell curl 5–8 reps

LEG PRESS

Focus: Quadriceps, hamstrings

Procedure: Place your feet at about hip-width on the pressing surface. Lower the weight until the knee-joint angle is 90 degrees and then press to the starting position.

Variations: Change feet positions—wide for more work on the inner thigh, narrow placement for emphasis on the outer thigh.

Training tip: Try to keep your feet flat on the pressing surface throughout the entire movement.

Related exercise: One-legged leg press

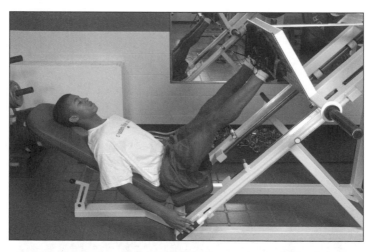

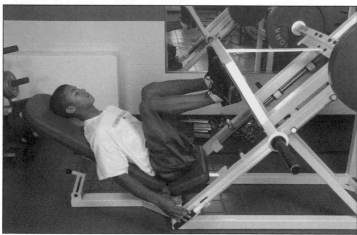

SQUAT

Focus: Quadriceps, glutes, upper hamstrings, and spinal erectors

Procedure: Place the bar along the top of your trapezius. Foot placement should be about shoulder-width. With your back straight, descend until the knee-joint angle is 90 degrees and then rise to the starting position.

Training tip: When starting to descend, try to keep your knees from moving forward. Keep your feet flat on the ground throughout the entire movement.

LUNGE

Focus: Quadriceps, hamstrings, glutes

Procedure: Foot placement is the same as that used for the squat. Lunging on the left leg begins by moving the right leg behind and maintaining a straight back while bending at your waist and descending. When the knee-joint angle is 90 degrees, rise to the starting position.

Variation: Step forward instead of behind.

Training tip: Keep your knees from moving forward when descending into the lunge position.

Related exercise: Dumbbell lunge

CLEAN DEADLIFT

Focus: Spinal erectors, glutes, hamstrings, quadriceps

Procedure: Place your feet at hip-width. Grip the bar slightly wider than shoulder-width. The bar should almost be touching your shins. With your back straight and knees above 90 degrees, begin rising with the bar using both your legs and your lower back. When you reach full extension, lower the bar to the ground following the same lifting path.

Training tips: To ensure that technique is correct, someone should watch from the side as you perform the lift. The observer will be looking to see that your hips move the same distance and speed as your shoulders do. Also, your legs should not straighten before your back is at full extension.

Related exercise: Dumbbell deadlift

Note: This lift is highly technical and requires an expert to teach and supervise the movement. Do not attempt to perform this lift without proper instruction and supervision.

CLEAN PULL

Focus: Spinal erectors, glutes, hamstrings, quadriceps, and vertical force

Procedure: The starting position is the same as that used for the clean deadlift. After lifting the bar from the ground, move the bar at a controlled and constant rate until it is about midthigh. When you reach midthigh, aggressively extend your body vertically and continue to pull the bar to about chest height.

Training tip: While jumping vertically, keep your arms straight when shrugging your shoulders and trapezius before pulling the bar with your arms.

HYPEREXTENSION

Focus: Spinal erectors, glutes, hamstrings

Procedure: Adjust the apparatus so that the pad lies directly against your quadriceps. While focusing on your hamstrings and glutes, raise your upper body until it is in alignment with your lower body. Slowly lower and repeat.

Training tip: Keep the motion slow and deliberate in both directions.

BENCH PRESS

Focus: Pectoralis major, anterior deltoid, triceps

Procedure: Lying on a flat bench, grip the bar wider than shoulder-width. Remove the bar from the uprights and start with the bar at straight arm's length. Lower the bar to the midsternum area, touch, and press back to the starting position.

Variations: You can perform this movement on a vertical or horizontal machine. A wider-than-normal grip will emphasize the outer pectoralis and the anterior deltoid. A grip narrower than normal will work the inner chest and triceps.

Training tips: Do not bounce the bar off your chest or arch your back, raising your glutes off the bench, in an effort to complete the lift. Doing so will place undue stress on other parts of your body and will likely cause injury.

Related exercise: Dumbbell bench press

INCLINE PRESS

Focus: Pectoralis minor, anterior deltoid, triceps

Procedure: Sitting on a 45-degree incline bench, grip the bar wider than shoulder-width. Remove the bar from the uprights and start with the bar at straight arm's length. Lower the bar to your clavicles, touch, and press back to the starting position.

Variation: You can also perform this movement on a machine.

Training tips: Do not bounce the bar off your chest or arch your back, raising your glutes off the bench, in an effort to complete the lift. Doing so will place undue stress on other parts of your body and will likely cause injury.

Related exercise: Dumbbell incline press

MILITARY PRESS

Focus: Anterior deltoid, lateral deltoid, triceps

Procedure: Seated or standing, begin with the bar resting on the front of your shoulders with a grip wider than shoulder-width. Press the bar overhead to full arm extension and return to the starting position.

Variation: You can also perform this movement on a machine.

Training tips: If you perform this movement standing, bend your knees slightly to relieve pressure from your lower back. Try not to lean back excessively when the movement becomes difficult. When you lean back, your pectorals come into use, muscles that are not the focus of this exercise.

Related exercise: Dumbbell military press

DUMBBELL LATERAL RAISE

Focus: Lateral head of the deltoid

Procedure: In a standing position, take two dumbbells and place them in front of your body on your thighs. Slightly bend your knees and bend at your waist while keeping your back straight. With your elbows slightly bent, raise the dumbbells out laterally, keeping your elbows higher than the dumbbells until your elbows reach shoulder height. Return to the starting position and repeat.

Variation: You can also perform this movement on a machine or with a pulley system.

Training tips: When raising the dumbbells, keep your palms facing down to emphasize the lateral head of the deltoid. You can also perform this movement with one arm per set.

DUMBBELL FRONT ALTERNATE RAISE

Focus: Anterior head of the deltoid

Procedure: Seated or standing, hold two dumbbells at the side of your thighs with your thumbs toward your body. Beginning with your right arm and your elbows slightly bent, raise the dumbbell to shoulder height. Lower and repeat with your left arm.

Variation: You can raise both dumbbells simultaneously or with a pulley system.

Training tip: Maintain your hand positioning throughout the movement.

BENT LATERAL RAISE

Focus: Posterior head of the deltoid

Procedure: For this exercise, keep your knees bent and your back parallel to the floor. With your arms slightly bent, raise the dumbbells out to the side until your shoulder blades meet. Lower and repeat.

Variations: You can perform this movement seated, with one arm per set, on a machine, or with a pulley system.

Training tips: Concentrate on raising the dumbbells by leading with your elbows. Always maintain bent elbows. Do not use your back to start the dumbbells moving up or to finish the movement.

DUMBBELL SHRUG

Focus: Trapezius

Procedure: Standing, grip the bar wider than shoulder-width. Shrug your shoulders as high as possible without bending your elbows. Lower and repeat.

Variation: You can also perform this movement on machinery.

Training tips: The focus should always be on shrugging your shoulders, not on the weight you are holding.

Related exercise: Shrug without dumbbells

LAT PULLDOWN

Focus: Latissimus dorsi

Procedure: Grip the bar slightly wider than shoulder-width. Leaning back, pull the bar toward your clavicles. With the same tempo, return the bar along the same path to the starting position.

Variation: Use an attachment that will allow a narrow grip. One attachment has the palms facing in, and another has the palms facing away from the body.

Training tips: Initiate the pull by focusing on driving your elbows toward your body. You must not focus on the bar. Do not use excessive body movement while performing this exercise.

Related exercise: Lat pulldown with narrow grip

SEATED ROW

Focus: Latissimus dorsi

Procedure: Grip the bar handles at shoulder-width. With your chest out and back straight, begin leaning back and pulling the bar to your midsection. Return the bar along the same path and repeat.

Variations: You can perform this exercise with one arm per set. Exercise machines can substitute for this movement.

Training tips: Initiate the pull by focusing on driving your elbows toward your body. You must not focus on the bar. Do not use excessive body movement while performing this exercise.

DUMBBELL ROW

Focus: Latissimus dorsi

Procedure: Place your knee opposite the arm doing the pulling on a bench. The foot of your other leg should be firmly on the ground. Lean on the opposite arm but do not fully extend it. With your back flat and tight, pull the dumbbell to your waistline, lower, and repeat.

Variation: You can place both feet on the floor if you require more stability.

Training tips: Balancing the body is the key to being able to pull the maximum amount of weight properly. Do not bring the dumbbell to your chest. Focus on lifting your elbow, not raising the weight.

BARBELL CURL

Focus: Biceps

Procedure: Grip the barbell with a palms-up grip so that your hands are a little wider than your hips. Keeping your elbows at the side of your body, raise the weight to your shoulders, lower, and repeat.

Variations: You can vary the grip for comfort or use a cambered bar (e-z curl bar).

Training tip: Do not use excessive body movement to start the bar moving or to finish the movement.

ALTERNATE DUMBBELL CURL

Focus: Biceps

Procedure: Seated or standing, begin with the dumbbells at the side of your body with palms facing forward. Keeping your elbows at the side of your body, raise the dumbbell in your right hand up to your shoulder and return to the starting position. Repeat with your left arm and alternate until you have performed the desired number of repetitions.

Variations: Face your palms toward your body. Turn the dumbbell to the palms-facing-forward position while lifting toward your shoulder. You can also raise both dumbbells simultaneously.

Training tips: Complete the raising and lowering motion of one arm before starting the movement of the other arm. Do not use excessive body movement to start the bar moving or to finish the movement.

LYING TRICEPS EXTENSION

Focus: Triceps

Procedure: Lying face up on a bench, extend your arms fully to grasp the barbell at shoulder-width. Maintain the position of your elbows and lower the barbell behind the top of your head. Raise the bar to the starting position and repeat.

Training tips: To focus on the triceps, your elbows must remain stationary. Do not raise your glutes from the bench while performing the movement.

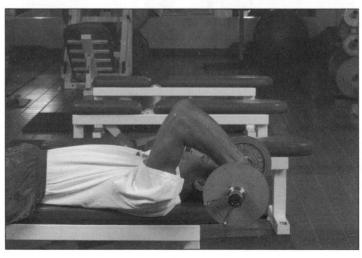

TRICEPS PUSHDOWN

Focus: Triceps

Procedure: Stand far enough away from the bar that a slight bend at the waist is necessary to address the bar. With your elbows at your side, grip the bar at shoulder-width and press the bar down to full extension. Return to the starting position and repeat.

Variation: You can substitute an attachment with a slight downward angle or a rope.

Training tip: Focus on your triceps and resist using your chest and shoulders to complete the movement.

LEG EXTENSION

Focus: Quadriceps, particularly the vastus medialis

Procedure: Comfortably place your feet so that the bottom part of your shin is in contact with the lever arm. Contract your quadriceps and raise the lever arm until your legs are just short of full extension. Lower and repeat.

Training tips: The starting position should not be less than 90 degrees. Do not use the momentum of your whole body to swing the weight up and down.

Related exercise: One-legged leg extension

LEG CURL

Focus: Hamstrings

Procedure: Place your feet under the lever arm so that the back of your leg, not any part of your foot, is in contact. Contract your hamstrings and raise the lever arm to your glutes. Lower and repeat.

Training tips: Do not use your whole body to initiate the movement. Do not raise your buttocks in an effort to finish the movement.

Related exercise: One-legged leg curl

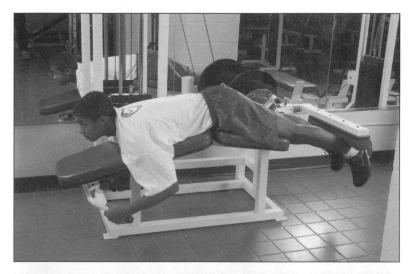

SEATED CALF RAISE

Focus: Soleus

Procedure: With knees bent at 90 degrees, lower your heels as far as possible and, without pausing, lift your heels as high as possible to contract your soleus. Lower and repeat.

Variation: You can also do this exercise with one leg.

Training tips: Try not to pull the machine with your arms to finish the movement. Pause for one count at the top of the movement to intensify the contraction.

Related exercise: One-legged seated calf raise

STANDING CALF RAISE

Focus: Gastrocnemius, soleus

Procedure: With your legs straight, lower your heels as far as possible and, without pausing, lift your heels as high as possible to contract your gastrocnemius. Lower and repeat.

Variation: You can also do this exercise with one leg.

Training tips: Try not to bend at the knees to push the weight up to finish the movement. Pause for one count at the top of the movement to intensify the contraction.

Related exercise: One-legged standing calf raise

CHAPTER 4

POWER TRAINING

Athletes in many sports do strength training in various forms, and soccer athletes today are much more likely to be involved in strength training than they were in the past. Although strength training is valuable, nothing is more important than the conversion of strength into power. Strength by itself has little to do with most sporting movements; absolute strength is forceful but slow. In soccer, power is involved in most of the movements that determine the difference between winning and losing.

Many terms and definitions describe power. Some of the interchangeable vocabulary includes these terms and phrases: ballistic, dynamic, powerful, explosive, speed-strength, producing the greatest possible force in the shortest period. Examples of actions in soccer that rely on power include short sprints, jumping, diving, quick shots on goal, long throw-ins, rapid acceleration from different running speeds, quick changes of direction, and punts downfield by the goalie.

As stated earlier, power should be the ultimate goal in refining training. For our purposes there are four ways to improve power— Olympic-style lifts, speed improvement, strength training, and plyometrics.

Olympic-style lifts have been calculated to be the most powerful movements a human can produce. The amount of work done in a short amount of time demonstrates exactly what power is all about. The movements from the ground in these lifts work the very muscles that are important for soccer—lower back, glutes, hamstrings, and quadriceps. Specifically, Olympic-style lifts help increase vertical jump, train explosiveness at the start of short sprints, and increase running speed by explosively strengthening the lower back, glutes, and hamstrings.

Speed improvement is a way of improving power! Speed improvement can be the result of several different training methods. Overall strengthening of the lower body along with the Olympic-style lifts, squats, and so on is one effective method. Second, improving the economy of the running motion by focusing on running mechanics will result in a faster run. Poor running technique is often the reason that strong, well-conditioned athletes cannot run fast. Correcting improper arm carry, body lean, and stride length are all certain ways to increase speed and subsequently power. Last, superior conditioning makes it easier to sprint and jump repeatedly and to make rapid changes of direction at full speed. During a match the action can become intense and furious, allowing little rest. The highly conditioned player will be able to maintain higher power output longer even though rest is at a minimum.

An athlete can increase power in only two ways—by getting faster or getting stronger. Strength training the entire body will result in higher power output. Although the lower body performs most of the work during all-out running, the upper body also plays an important role. When the body becomes stronger, speed increases, vertical jump increases, and strength-endurance increases to permit a longer period of higher output. Jeff Agoos of the Earthquakes and Joe-Max Moore of the US National Team are examples of a powerful defender and attacker, respectively.

Plyometric training is a familiar topic to coaches and athletes involved with the teaching and learning of explosiveness. Plyometrics has been defined as a type of exercise that bridges the gap between strength and speed. Obviously, then, plyometrics can be valuable in a program designed to promote speed, explosiveness, and power. By definition, plyometric exercises are designed to stress the stretch reflex in the muscle to speed up the neuromuscular response. The speed of the stretch is important, not the magnitude. As an example, you will notice that squatting deeply before jumping does not produce nearly the result that a shorter, quicker jump can. On the other hand, top speed does not always produce the most powerful movement. Touching your forefinger to your thumb at top speed is fast but not forceful. The blending of top speed and strength produces the best movement.

Plyometric exercises can be used for both upper- and lower-body training. As specificity allows, we will be spending our time on lower-body plyometrics for obvious reasons. Most of the exercises revolve around jumping and hopping on one or both legs—vertically, horizontally, or a combination of both.

HOW PLYOMETRICS HELPS THE SOCCER ATHLETE

We will identify three ways in which plyometrics can improve the soccer athlete's skills.

Improving speed. Sprinting, striding, and some jumping are essentially a series of one-legged hops. In reality, movement in any direction for any distance requires one-legged executions. Plyometrics, combined with the strength gained by weightlifting, will teach the legs how to respond with great force in a short period. You will begin to understand that jumping, hopping, and bounding contribute to creating speed in any direction. Unlike a track-oriented program, plyometrics for soccer can significantly improve the speed of movement in more than one direction.

Improving balance. Hurdling, hopping, and jumping over objects require balance for proper execution. Changing directions rapidly while dribbling or marking would be almost impossible without good balance. Plyometrics, whether performed with one or two legs, will force the body to learn balance and at the same time create strength in a balanced position. This training has a carryover effect to the most fundamental soccer actions—jumping, heading, tackling, striking, and positioning.

Training for explosiveness. Explosiveness here refers to rapid acceleration or a quick change of direction. The ability to attain speed from a dead stop is demonstrated when a back-to-the-goal attacker turns and sprints to the near post for a shot on goal. The player who jumps for a punted ball at midfield in a group of defenders must jump vertically as fast and high as possible. Changing direction at any speed with little delay occurs when a wing jogs slowly down the sideline and then breaks at full speed to the goal for a cross ball. Rapid acceleration from different running speeds is required when a defender moves slowly into position, then marks an opponent without the ball, and then sprints as an attacker tries to reach a free ball in the corner.

Plyometric drills combine speed and strength, enabling the athlete to move quickly from a dead stop or accelerate in any direction at any speed.

HOW TO MAKE PLYOMETRICS EFFECTIVE

Randomly performing plyometrics without any attention to progression, technique, or conditioning will result only in injury and frustration. If you want your plyometric program to work, you must consider three major points.

Strength training. We hope by now you see that becoming stronger is essential to success in soccer. Earlier we discussed how important strength is to becoming more explosive. Strength is equally important in reducing injury while performing plyometrics. Leg strength is critical to avoiding injury to the knees, ankles, and lower back. Because plyometric movements are ballistic, a certain strength base is essential to prevent injuries as well as gain optimum benefits. Some data have indicated that an athlete should be able to squat between 1.5 to 2.0 times her body weight before engaging in a plyometrics program. But we feel that if a lower-body strength program is in place, the training should bring about positive changes in speed and explosiveness. Do not consider a plyometric program without a solid lower-body strength program and a comprehensive conditioning schedule. All three components must be present.

Reducing the risk of injury. The following list of rules should help prevent serious injury to soccer athletes who perform plyometrics:

1. Athletes must not ignore any aches or pains in the lower back, knees, ankles, or feet. A certified health professional should evaluate the pain before the athlete continues.

2. To help absorb landing forces, players should wear a sturdy training shoe with a solid midsole and forefoot construction.

3. Athletes should perform a thorough flexibility routine and warm-up before training (see chapter 2).

4. Make sure the landing surface is resilient. Portable mats or grassy areas are acceptable surfaces. Gymnasium floors are not.

5. Do not begin a plyometric workout schedule without the benefit of a comprehensive training program.

6. Preadolescent athletes should avoid plyometrics because of the stress on immature bones and connective tissues. Strength at this age will be sufficient for increasing speed and power without the use of plyometrics.

Using proper technique. Technique for any exercise is important, particularly when athletes are working on creating power. For speed of movement, proper positioning, and injury prevention, athletes must observe certain performance parameters.

1. Players should land with as little flexion as possible at the ankles, knees, and waist. Too much flexion means too much time on the ground, which translates into reduced reaction time and speed of movement.

2. For explosion, balance, and reaction, athletes should use their arms aggressively.

3. Players must rest between sets for proper recovery. Plyometrics is a high-quality exercise. Players should not be fatigued while performing the drills.

4. Athletes should maintain a position of balance from the beginning of the movement to the end.

5. Drills should be closely related to soccer movements, including speed and change of direction.

DESIGNING A PLYOMETRIC PROGRAM

By understanding the components and planning behind a plyometric program, you will be able to make minor adjustments and personalize a program to fit the needs of each athlete.

Frequency

If designed, implemented, and evaluated correctly, two plyometric workouts per week will be sufficient. This schedule should remain unchanged throughout the training year. Other parts of the program might vary, such as the number of repetitions or the menu of drills, but the frequency should remain unchanged. Avoid plyometrics on days that include medium- to high-intensity weight training, cardiovascular work, or running. The speed and quality of work necessary to perform plyometrics will be compromised if drills are performed on days with high activity levels. If for some reason plyometric exercises are performed on a day that includes other strenuous workouts, make certain that the drills are the first task of the day's work after a thorough flexibility and warm-up period.

Volume

Many programs make recommendations for volume (number of repetitions and sets) in a workout. Not much has been done in terms of soccer, so the best indicator of effectiveness remains personal and individual evaluation. We see many different programs in sports because coaches seek what works best in their situations. Although some guidelines for design exist, the program should eventually be modified through evaluation and experience. Conservatism is the best place to begin when establishing volume. History has proved that most programs call for excessive volume. Remember, the combination and cumulative effect of all training components are what make plyometrics effective. Athletes will benefit from conservative volume as long as it is large enough to stimulate a training effect and is in synchrony with other components.

Observe these guidelines for adjusting volumes:

1. Limit training sets to three to five.

2. To preserve the quality of the drills, raise the volume by increasing the number of sets, not the number of repetitions.

3. The complexity of the drill and the degree of fatigue it causes determine the number of repetitions per set. A repetition range of three to six is acceptable.

Intensity

Unlike weight training or timed running, plyometric drills are not easily assigned an intensity (with a percentage) that indicates effort. Intensity for a plyometric drill is based on the difficulty of the movement. For example, a one-legged triple jump has a higher intensity than a two-legged standing long jump. The drill progression and yearly schedule will determine what drill to perform at each time of year. As with other components of training, general movements will dominate at the beginning of the year, and drills that are more specific will follow.

Duration

The length of time required to perform the drills is inconsequential. Execution of each movement depends on difficulty and volume. Special attention should be paid to rest periods between sets and drills. Abnormal fatigue (labored breathing, burning muscles) should never be present. Quality of effort is the principal factor in producing a beneficial workout. Because speed and proper mechanics are what produce power, fatigue is the enemy. Athletes must rest as long as necessary between sets to ensure 100 percent effort with good speed and mechanics.

Progression

The normal sequence begins with basic movements and progresses toward more difficult specific drills. Two-footed movements begin the yearly training cycle, with the objective to progress to one-legged movements. The rate of progress from two-legged to one-legged movements depends on the athlete. Speed of execution and proper technique are the primary indicators of progress. The more balance and speed displayed by the athlete, the quicker the progression occurs. The coach should evaluate these items during every workout.

The following list is ordered from beginning to advanced movements:

1. Two-legged, single response, in place—max vertical jump
2. Two-legged, multi-response, in place—double tuck jump
3. Two-legged, single response, moving—standing long jump
4. Two-legged, multi-response, moving—standing triple jump
5. One-legged, single response, in place—one-legged vertical jump
6. One-legged, multi-response, in place—double one-legged vertical jump
7. One-legged, single response, moving—one-legged standing long jump
8. One-legged, multi-response, moving—one-legged standing double jump
9. Two-legged, combination jump—vertical jump to a long jump
10. One-legged, combination jump—one-legged vertical jump to a one-legged long jump

LATERAL MOVEMENT PLYOMETRICS

Soccer is not solely a straight-ahead sport. The ability to move quickly left and right is a necessary weapon in an athlete's soccer arsenal.

SIDE TO SIDE, ONE-LEGGED OR TWO-LEGGED

Procedure: Determine the distance to travel laterally. Weaker, less conditioned athletes will require shorter distances. The beginning athlete can use a single line. Stand with your feet spaced at hip-width and with your knees slightly bent. Begin by hopping right, left, right, left, and so on with both feet, as fast as possible. Each touch of the ground is one repetition.

Performance tips: Speed of movement is the most important part of this drill. For the fastest pace, keep your body low to the ground and balanced in a fashion similar to that used by a skier moving side to side downslope. Use of the arms is important in producing explosive movement.

Variation: You can add a vertical component to work on jumping laterally over obstacles (for instance, a low bench or small cones).

Prescription: One to five sets of 10 repetitions, 6 to 36 inches (15 to 91 centimeters).

ANGLE HOP, ONE-LEGGED OR TWO-LEGGED

Procedure: Determine the distance to travel at 45-degree angles. Weaker, less conditioned athletes will require shorter distances. Stand with your feet spaced at hip-width and your knees slightly bent, facing forward. Jump to the right with both feet at a 45-degree angle, maintaining your body positioning forward. Immediately upon landing, jump to the left at a 45-degree angle and continue to repeat for the given distance.

Performance tips: For balance on landing and takeoff, keep your body low to the ground and your knees slightly bent. Use of the arms is important in producing explosive movement.

Variations: You can add a vertical component to work on jumping laterally over obstacles. Small obstacles can be placed between the landing points.

Prescription: One to five sets of 4 to 10 repetitions. Longer distances require fewer repetitions. The distance will be determined by your strength and conditioning.

VERTICAL MOVEMENT PLYOMETRICS

Explosive teams are adept at handling the ball in the air. An athlete that is sound in this dimension of the game gains the competitive edge.

MAX VERTICAL JUMP, ONE-LEGGED OR TWO-LEGGED

Procedure: Place your feet at hip-width with your arms at your sides. Jump as high as possible, aggressively using your arms and keeping them extended through the apex of the jump.

Performance tips: Use your arms aggressively and vertically. Good height on the jump depends on the quickness of the down-up movement before the jump.

Variations: Repeat max vertical jumps by performing a double max vertical jump (two consecutive jumps) or a triple max vertical jump (three consecutive jumps). Pause in the quarter-squat position for one second before the jump.

Prescription: One to five sets of 5 to 10 repetitions. Perform fewer repetitions for the repeat jumps (count one double jump as one repetition).

TUCK JUMP, ONE-LEGGED OR TWO-LEGGED

Procedure: Place your feet at hip-width with your arms at your sides. Jump as high as possible, aggressively using your arms and keeping them extended through the apex of the jump. At the apex of the jump, bring your knees to waist height and lower them before landing. During the tuck, you can move your arms in front of your body for balance.

Performance tip: Do not cut the jump short in an effort to tuck quickly. Maximum tuck is required for correct performance of the tuck.

Variations: Repeat tuck jumps by performing double jump tucks (two consecutive tuck jumps) or triple tuck jumps (three consecutive tuck jumps).

Prescription: One to five sets of 5 to 10 repetitions. Perform fewer repetitions for the repeat jumps (count one double jump as one repetition).

SQUAT JUMP

Procedure: Place your feet at hip-width with your arms at your sides. Descend into a half-squat position with your knee joint forming a 90-degree angle. When you reach the 90-degree angle, explode upward, using your arms aggressively.

Performance tip: Use your arms to balance your body while descending and ascending.

Variations: For pause squat jumps, hold the 90-degree-angle position for a one-second count before jumping vertically. For repeat squat jumps, perform double squat jumps (two consecutive squat jumps) or triple squat jumps (three consecutive squat jumps).

Prescription: One to five sets of 5 to 10 repetitions. Perform fewer repetitions for the repeat jumps (count one double jump as one repetition).

HORIZONTAL MOVEMENT PLYOMETRICS

Running dominates the game of soccer. A focus on horizontal movement adds explosiveness to an athlete's ability to change speeds quickly and sprint.

STANDING LONG JUMP, ONE-LEGGED OR TWO-LEGGED

Procedure: Place your feet at hip-width with your arms at your sides. Using your arms aggressively, jump forward as far as possible. Proper technique will allow you to land so that you do not fall backward.

Performance tip: Do not squat deeply before jumping. Doing so will slow your acceleration and limit the distance of your jump.

Variations: For pause standing long jumps, hold the takeoff position for a one-second count before jumping. For repeat standing long jumps, perform double standing long jumps (two consecutive standing long jumps) or triple standing long jumps (three consecutive standing long jumps).

Prescription: One to five sets, five repetitions. Perform fewer repetitions for the repeat jumps (count one double jump as one repetition).

OBSTACLE HOP, ONE-LEGGED OR TWO-LEGGED

Procedure: Objects (low hurdles, cones, etc.) are spaced evenly in a straight line in front of you. Hop over the objects for the prescribed distance or repetitions in a balanced athletic position.

Performance tip: Maintaining good balance when landing ensures a rhythmic jumping pattern.

Variations: Vary the height of the obstacles to simulate changing game situations.

Prescription: One to five sets, 3 to 10 repetitions (obstacles). Perform fewer repetitions for higher or longer jumps.

COMBINATION JUMP

A combination jump is an advanced set of jumps that combines two or more plyometric exercises in one repetition. These drills teach the body to react in more than one direction without resting between movements. You can be creative and design your own combinations, using these ideas as a starting point. Use the previously described procedures for the correct technical execution of the jumps.

- Vertical jump to a standing long jump
- Lateral hop left to a max vertical jump
- Repeat vertical jump to obstacle hop
- Squat jump to a standing long jump
- Obstacle hop to a standing long jump
- Lateral hop left to a max vertical jump, lateral hop right to a max vertical jump
- Standing long jump to a repeat tuck jump

CHAPTER 5

ENDURANCE TRAINING

Conditioning, or fitness as it is commonly known in the soccer world, has an unquestionable effect on an athlete. To begin a match or season without top fitness is to guarantee failure. So important is conditioning that some athletes use their fitness as a form of intimidation or as a strategy against an opponent. For instance, "runners" will use the entire pitch to wear down an opponent to the point where he is unable to defend.

Constant motion during a match involving various speeds, directions, and distances requires commitment to fitness training. The varying intensity of the game requires us to define what it takes to reach optimal levels of conditioning.

DEMANDS OF THE GAME

Aerobic and *anaerobic* are two terms that circulate when conditioning is the topic. The intent of this book is to avoid becoming too scientific about these energy sources, but coaches and athletes should have a basic understanding of the terms and how they apply to soccer.

Aerobic capacity is the ability to use oxygen during exercise. Aerobic pathways start in the same way that anaerobic pathways do, but because the intensity of the exercise is low (producing little or no lactic acid), oxygen is supplied and fat is the main energy source. By definition, aerobic exercise is performed at 60 to 80 percent of maximum heart rate for 20 to 40 minutes of uninterrupted exercise. Jogging or cycling at a moderate pace is an example of aerobic exercise. During a match, the recovery periods between sprinting or continuous movement offer time for the player to use aerobic pathways to return oxygen to the system.

Of course, soccer is not always played at low intensity. Changes of speed and stop-and-go action are often explosive and aggressive. But a good aerobic base is the foundation that leads to speed, speed-endurance, and the ability to change speeds repeatedly. Although the aerobic energy system has low power output, developing a base early in a program

- increases the work capacity of the body as a unit,
- improves the working efficiency of the heart and lungs,
- increases the body's ability to use oxygen, and
- prepares the body for higher intensity work without risk of injury, staleness, or rapid fatigue.

Anaerobic capacity is the ability to perform repetitive, intense activity with little or no rest. As you might guess this all occurs in the absence of oxygen. This type of activity produces elevated fatigue in a short time. Aerobic training is not intense enough to have an effect on this energy source, so soccer athletes need to train specifically to match the intensity of anaerobic work and the demand that it places on the body. Work-rest interval training at medium to high intensity is the exercise mode that most efficiently taxes this system. We will discuss this topic later in this chapter.

Although aerobic training is not the key to endurance performance, it must be integrated with an anaerobic component in a complete approach to conditioning. The athlete who successfully completes a program and achieves an acceptable level of fitness can realize several advantages:

- Ability to change speed over long distances with less fatigue
- Ability to maintain top speed for a longer period
- Capacity to maintain skills (passing, shooting, receiving)
- Ability to maintain concentration because of the absence of fatigue

AEROBIC CONDITIONING

Running is a way of life for the soccer athlete. Because a great deal of running occurs during the season, only a limited amount of running for aerobic training is necessary during this time. In-season, stationary bikes, steppers, rowing machines, and the like should be the equipment of choice for one or two workouts per week. Remember that on most days the athlete receives a certain amount of fitness training in practice sessions.

Off-season, runs of up to 30 minutes early in the training process can build a foundation for more intense activity to come. Other appropriate off-season activities are swimming, basketball, and recreational soccer.

Aerobic exercises should be between 20 and 40 minutes of uninterrupted movement at a heart rate between 60 and 80 percent of maximum heart rate. Keep in mind that the exercise time starts only when the heart rate reaches the appropriate range.

Aerobic workouts can be performed with several modes of exercise:

Lifecycle

Level 3, 85 to 90 rpm for 5 minutes

Levels 5 to 7, 85 to 90 rpm for 20 to 40 minutes

Treadmill

Walk 0 percent grade, 3.0 to 4.0 mph for 5 minutes

Jog 0 percent grade, 5.5 to 7.5 mph for 20 to 30 minutes

Stairmaster

Levels 4 to 6 for 5 minutes

Levels 8 to 12 for 20 to 40 minutes

ANAEROBIC CONDITIONING

Training to develop anaerobic capacity is more diverse and lends itself to creativity. The most effective way to increase anaerobic capacity (strength-endurance, speed-endurance, power-endurance) and at the same time affect the aerobic pathways is the work-rest nature of interval training.

Interval training offers several advantages over typical low-intensity endurance work:

- Higher intensity of exercise
- Ability to do a significantly greater amount of work by breaking up the total work into short bouts with full or shortened recovery periods
- Generation of greater energy for a longer period
- Ability to produce gamelike intensity

Sets, repetitions, distances or times, and rest intervals are the variables manipulated to vary the intensity and the result. To discover what works best might take some time. For instance, it is easy to find interval-training programs for 400-meter runners, but how do they apply to soccer athletes of various ages, sizes, and training levels? The best way to test a program is to implement it. Over time the best drills will emerge.

In soccer, running is of obvious importance and should make up the majority of the training. Professional players run miles during the course of a game. Stationary bicycles, steppers, rowing machines, and treadmills can easily be administered as interval-training apparatus. If the work time and rest time are measured, then the intensity (resistance or difficulty) can be adjusted to obtain the desired results.

The two forms of straight-ahead running we will use in the interval-training samples are stride intervals and sprint intervals. Stride technique involves using a longer-than-normal stride but running with 100 percent effort. Because of the exaggerated stride length, the speed will be 75 to 85 percent of normal sprint speed. Sprint technique is 100 percent effort at 100 percent speed. In other words, the athlete runs as hard and fast as possible.

Sample Interval-Training Programs

Stride interval training

8 strides × 80 yards (73 meters) with :24 rest

1:30 rest

8 strides × 40 yards (37 meters) with :12 rest

1:30 rest

8 strides × 20 yards (18 meters) with :06 rest

Sprint interval training

6 sprints × 30 yards (27 meters) with :27 rest

3:00 rest

6 sprints × 15 yards (14 meters) with :15 rest

3:00 rest

10 sprints × 5 yards (5 meters) with :07 rest

Combination stride-sprint interval training

6 strides × 100 yards (91 meters) with :30 rest

1:30 rest

6 strides × 60 yards (55 meters) with :18 rest

1:30 rest

8 sprints × 10 yards (9 meters) with :06 rest

Lifecycle interval training

5 minutes at level 4 at 90 rpm

20 minutes, alternating between level 6 for :45 and

level 9 for :15 at 80 rpm

Other Applications of Interval Training

As noted earlier, movement in soccer is not solely straight ahead. Specific conditioning drills can improve players' ability to move from side to side, to change direction, and to change speed. Incorporating gamelike activities will make the conditioning program more relevant to soccer. Agility drills with or without the ball are excellent opportunities to incorporate soccerlike interval training. Dribbling, shooting, or passing drills executed with a given number of repetitions and limited rest mimic soccer movements and at the same time condition the athletes. Agility drills based on time enable athletes to learn what it is like to explode repetitively and react with minimal rest.

CHAPTER 6

AGILITY TRAINING

Balance, strength, coordination,

and endurance are all necessary components of agility. To be able to change direction at speeds of 50 to 100 percent effort with different body angles while dribbling with alternating feet requires many physical qualities. To a certain degree, agility is an inherent skill. Nevertheless, players can greatly improve their agility.

Agility as it applies to soccer is the physical ability to change movements quickly in the unpredictable, ever-changing game environment. Sometimes confused with the term *coordination*, agility is more than becoming efficient in certain movement patterns. Because the sudden change in movement is brought on by the unforeseeable, agility is also a measure of the ability to limit the time between the decision for the new movement and the execution of the movement. As you can see, the measure of an athlete's agility includes more than the ability to jump over a cone. For example, a moderate display of agility would be dribbling past a defender in a one-on-one situation. A high level of agility is demonstrated by a defender marking an opponent who steals the ball from a different oncoming offensive player, dribbles through two or three opposing players, and then chooses a target downfield to pass to. As the number of variables increases, so does the difficulty. In summary, agility requires the ability to change movement patterns rapidly while encountering unpredictable situations, make quick decisions, and act on them in a timely and efficient manner.

For the soccer athlete, agility training is perfect for increasing skill levels. In a soccer match, varying degrees of agility occur at different parts of the pitch at the same time. Many things are happening on the ball and away from the ball, and at a moment's notice the atmosphere can change from one side of the pitch to the other! The changing environment of soccer necessitates quick decision making. Improving agility will improve soccer skills. It's that simple.

Clear definitions of the key elements of agility will explain how the outlined drills can help develop the fully conditioned soccer athlete.

change of direction—Moving from one path of direction to another by one step or more. The true test of directional change occurs at high speeds, combining various changes, one after another. There is nothing as exciting as watching Marco Etcheverry take charge of the offense by spinning, turning, and jostling while eluding a defender in the corner.

coordination—Organized muscular action in executing complex movements. Developing the skills to hurdle obstacles, change direction, and maneuver in the air enhances coordination. Performing these complex movements and drills and then changing the conditions or complexity will carry over into improved agility.

decision making—Recognizing when, where, and how to make changes in movement pattern will come with experience. Performing coordination drills, agility drills, and learning under gamelike conditions will improve the decision-making process by instilling familiarity.

fitness—Performing drills that will lead to a higher level of agility stresses the body. Optimal fitness and strength allow the athlete to train hard while executing the drills. If fatigue is present during training, the athlete will perform the drills improperly, resulting in meaningless effort. The athlete who is not well conditioned also faces a higher risk of injury during training and matches.

Drills to improve movement are simpler than most people believe. Concentrating on basic movement patterns and becoming proficient with them will lead to better application and execution of those movements during a match.

Agility drills can be done year-round, but the volume should vary throughout the year. In the off-season, players should perform drills two or three times per week. In-season, practice time is dedicated to skills and strategies, so the drills should be limited to once or twice per week.

FOUR CORNERS

Objective: To develop change of direction capability at any speed or distance with correct mechanics

Procedure: Face in one direction during the entire drill. (1) Sprint forward. (2) Move left by pushing off on your right foot to a lateral heel-to-heel slide, with no crossover. (3) Backpedal by pushing backward on your left foot. (4) Move right by pushing off on your left foot to a lateral heel-to-heel slide, with no crossover. When you reach the cone at the starting point, repeat in the opposite direction without pausing. Completing the drill in both directions is one repetition.

Volume: Place cones 3 to 10 yards (3 to 9 meters) apart. Perform 5 to 10 repetitions for three to five sets with adequate rest between repetitions to allow proper execution of the drill. Shorter rest periods will result in a better conditioning effect.

Variations: (1) For more endurance-oriented results, add more size to the square. (2) For more speed work, use a smaller square. (3) Alter the speed variations by changing the square into a rectangle, using the long side for the lateral work or the sprint and backpedal portion. (4) Including a ball at each change of direction will allow the player to strike, pass, or head the ball.

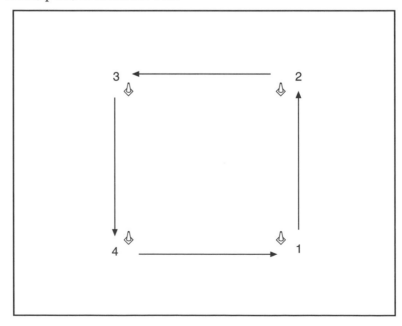

LATERAL SHUFFLE

Objective: To develop lateral conditioning, movement, and change of direction

Procedure: Face in one direction during the entire drill. (1) Laterally move to the left with a heel-to-heel slide, with no crossover. (2) Plant on your left foot and move to the right. Moving from right to left is one repetition.

Volume: Place cones 3 to 15 yards (3 to 14 meters) apart. Perform 10 to 20 repetitions for 5 to 10 sets with adequate rest between repetitions to allow proper execution of the drill. Shorter rest periods will result in a better conditioning effect.

Variations: (1) For more endurance-oriented results, add more distance to the drill. (2) For more speed work, use shorter distances. (3) Performing the drill in an exaggerated squat will emphasize the quadriceps. (4) Including a ball at each change of direction will allow the player to strike, pass, or head the ball.

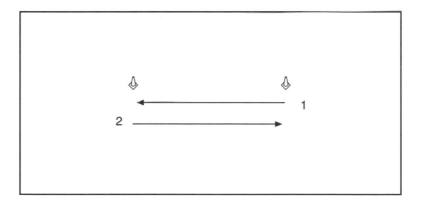

FORWARD AND BACKWARD

Objective: To develop the ability to change direction from forward to backward. This transition is difficult at above-average speeds, so players must practice proper body positioning and footwork.

Procedure: Face in one direction during the entire drill. (1) Sprint forward. (2) Backpedal. When driving into the backpedal, take as few steps as possible during the transition. A sprint and backpedal are one repetition.

Volume: Place cones 3 to 15 yards (3 to 14 meters) apart. Perform the drill for 5 to 10 repetitions for 5 to 10 sets with adequate rest between repetitions to allow proper execution of the drill. Shorter rest periods will result in a better conditioning effect.

Variations: (1) For more endurance-oriented results, add distance to the drill. (2) For more speed work, use shorter distances.

A variation for both the lateral shuffle and the forward-backward drill is to use an auditory cue to indicate the change of direction. The coach can use the cue—a whistle, horn, or clap—at any time to vary the distance of work and add an element of reaction.

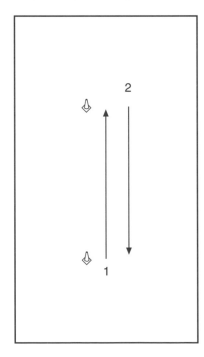

LATERAL SNAKE

Objective: To develop footwork and balance in a lateral or forward direction

Procedure: Place a series of cones in a straight line, spaced evenly. Face in one direction during the entire drill. (1) Without crossing over with your feet, slide heel to heel to the right, past cone #1. (2) Plant your right foot and drive forward past cone #2. (3) Plant your left foot and slide heel to heel to the right, past cone #2. (4) Plant your right foot and drive into a backpedal past cone #2. (5) Plant your left foot and slide heel to heel to the right, past cone #3. Repeat this procedure for the entire distance. Perform the drill in both directions for one repetition.

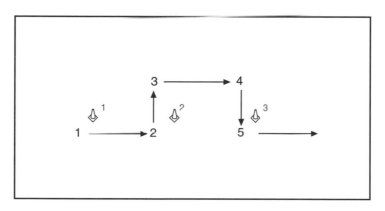

RUN-AND-CUT SNAKE

Procedure: Place a series of cones in a straight line, evenly spaced. Face in one direction during the entire drill. (1) Starting to the right side of cone #1, run to cone #2. (2) Plant your right foot and drive to the left, past cone #2. (3) Plant your left foot and run forward past cone #2. (4) Plant your left foot and drive laterally before cone #3, past cone #2. Do not cross over on the lateral movements. (5) Repeat for the entire drill.

Volume: Place cones one to five yards apart. Perform the drill for 10 to 20 cones for 5 to 10 sets with adequate rest between repetitions to allow proper execution. Shorter rest periods will result in a better conditioning effect.

Variations: Changing the distance between the cones will alter speed, determining the conditioning effect and the complexity of the foot-work. For instance, with the cones one yard apart, speed will be lower but footwork will be more challenging. When the cones are placed five yards apart, speed increases and significant conditioning effect occurs.

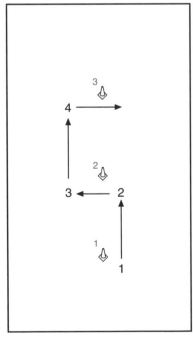

FIGURE 8

Objective: To improve footwork and change-of-direction capability at angles other than 90 degrees

Procedure: Set up the drill as you did the four-corners drill. (1) Beginning at cone #4 at the bottom right of the square, sprint forward to cone #2. (2) Plant your left foot and slide to the right toward cone #1, heel to heel, with no crossover. (3) Plant your right foot, turn, and run toward cone #3. (4) Plant your right foot and slide to the left, toward cone #4, heel to heel, with no crossover.

Volume: Place cones five yards apart. Perform the drill for 5 to 10 repetitions and three to five sets.

Variations: (1) Face in one direction for the entire drill as if watching the ball or defenders. (2) Face a new direction on each route. (3) Vary the movement mechanics on each route (for example, slide-backpedal-sprint-sprint). (4) Include a ball at each change of direction for striking, passing, or heading.

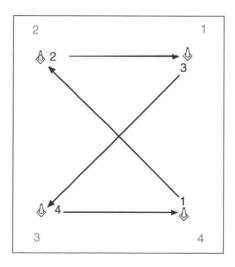

V DRILL

Purpose: To emphasize 45-degree angle turns

Procedure: Place three cones to form a 45-degree angle. (1) Sprint forward to the left cone, #1. (2) At cone #1, plant your right foot and backpedal toward the starting point. (3) Without pause, repeat steps 1 and 2 in the opposite direction. A sprint and backpedal in both directions are one repetition.

Volume: Place cones 3 to 10 yards (3 to 9 meters) apart. Perform the drill for 5 to 10 repetitions and three to five sets with adequate rest between repetitions to allow proper execution. Shorter rest periods will result in a better conditioning effect.

Variations: (1) Change mechanics of the run each time (for example, slide and sprint the first length instead of sprinting and backpedaling). (2) Add a ball to the drill for striking, passing, or heading.

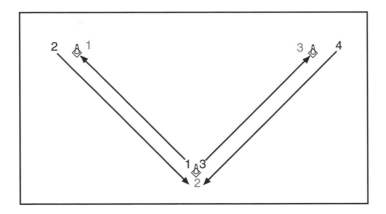

ALPHABET MOVEMENT

Purpose: To improve change of direction in any direction

Procedure: Choose any capital letter of the alphabet constructed with straight lines (for example, A, E, F, H, and so on). (1) Begin at the bottom right of the letter. (2) Determine direction. (3) Determine movement mechanics—backpedal, sprint, or slide. (4) Determine repetition and rest interval. The more complex the drill, the fewer the repetitions and the longer the rest periods.

For example, with the letter L use this sequence: (1) Slide left five yards to cone #2, with no crossover. (2) From cone #2 sprint forward to cone #3. (3) Backpedal from cone #3 to cone #2. (4) Plant your right foot at cone #2 and slide, with no crossover, to cone #1. This sequence is one repetition.

Volume: The number of repetitions and sets depends on the size of the letter and the number of movements involved.

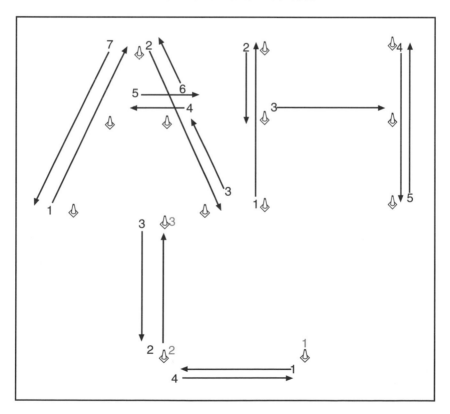

CHAPTER 7

SPEED TRAINING

When coaches talk about the qualities they find endearing in an athlete, speed is usually at the top of the list. Determination, strength, fitness, and skills are important, but speed is the commodity that can change the course of a match all by itself!

Running speed can easily be evaluated by timing athletes over a given distance or comparing one athlete to another in a race. But speed relevant to soccer is not necessarily detectable by watching a player outrun an opponent. Straight-line speed is only one display of speed in the sport. Speed for our purpose includes the ability to react quickly, change direction on a dime, change speeds, and repeatedly perform these tasks at a consistently high level throughout a match. Aside from one-on-one matchups, think about what speed does to the scope of a match. The defense is always under pressure, always concerned about the athletes who possess speed. When the defense focuses on one or two key players, the field begins to open up for others. Players with speed force the defense to design their plan around them!

Offensively, scoring opportunities increase, and the number of attacks designed around speed begins to grow. Kick and run becomes a simple but effective method for scoring. Teams with speed can pursue high-risk defensive schemes because their ability to recover means that small mistakes won't be disastrous. Conversely, an offense that lacks speed is also a defense that lacks speed. Without speed, the game plan changes significantly.

What speed can do for an athlete, team, or organization should not be understated. The main obstacle in the path of acquiring speed is commitment. Although we often talk about speed, coaches typically do not set aside time during practice to focus on improving game speed. Athletes and coaches alike must understand that every athlete can become faster with applied effort.

COMPONENTS OF SOCCER SPEED

Words like *explosive* and *quick* are used interchangeably when discussing the speed of athletes. These qualities are important if you are a forward accelerating past a defender, a midfielder initiating an overlapping run, or a defender recovering during a breakaway. We now know that the words *explosive* and *quick* are describing power. Now is the time to begin to define speed accurately. To determine soccer-relevant speed, we must first identify the components. Speed in relation to soccer involves (a) strength, (b) endurance (fitness), (c) ability to change direction, (d) reaction time, and (e) running mechanics.

Strength

Strength is crucial for many reasons:

- To build endurance, strength levels must be optimal.
- Strength is a component of power (speed).
- Strength is necessary to reduce the risk of injury that is associated with the intensity of sprint training, interval training, plyometrics, and gamelike conditions.
- Increase in stride length is closely associated with an increase in leg strength.

The foundation of all physical movement begins with strength. The athlete who lacks strength will not benefit significantly from the training involved in improving speed. A great deal of strength is not required to change direction, but it does take a large amount of strength to change direction quickly and precisely (for example, to dribble left, dribble right, and then shoot on goal). Strength is necessary to change running speed from slow to fast over a short distance; weaker athletes need more time to reach top speed. Stronger athletes will be able to work on improving speed with less risk of injury. Chapter 3 describes strength-training programs that will help soccer players become stronger.

Endurance

A proper strength and conditioning program will improve several aspects of endurance:

- Ability to change speeds repetitively and continuously
- Maintenance of speed over both long and short distances
- Maintenance of proper running mechanics for a longer period
- Ability to run repetitively at top speed with minimum rest between bursts
- Reduction in injuries related to top-speed running and ballistic movements

In this case, speed-endurance and strength-endurance are the fitness components associated with speed. Game fitness, the minimum requirement for success, is met by normal training, practices, and matches. Training for speed requires an accelerated and aggressive approach to fitness. Chapter 5 on endurance training discusses ways to improve fitness.

Ability to Change Direction Rapidly

A change of direction is effective only if it is performed rapidly. Dribbling a ball past midfield into a congested defense requires multiple changes of direction while dribbling with both feet. Movements must be sudden, quick, and repetitive. The great ball handlers like Bebeto or Renaldo of Brazil change direction quickly and sharply. Although most directional changes occur in a five-yard perimeter, an element of speed and endurance remains that only a strong, powerful athlete can produce. If there is a lack of strength, there is no sharpness. Lack of fitness means that crisp repetition of movement cannot occur. By combining

strength, endurance, a plyometric program, and the agility drills from chapter 6, the soccer athlete can develop tremendous ability to change direction.

Reaction Time

Performing a drill repeatedly can produce accurate movements. But during a match the athlete encounters nothing as predictable as a drill. This is where minimizing reaction time is critical for success. Reaction time in soccer depends on visual stimuli that the athlete processes to make decisions. Reaction time begins when the thought for action occurs and ends when the action is complete. When a defender attempts a tackle, the ball handler's reaction time determines whether he keeps possession of the ball. The goalkeeper's reaction time in defending a two-on-one determines whether the result is a stop or a goal. When a player is in position to take a shot on goal, a teammate may break free by the near post. The reaction time of the player with the ball governs whether he passes the ball or shoots. Three basic parameters influence reaction time—the environment that causes the thought for action, the time between the thought for action and the initiation of action, and the time between the initiation of action and its completion. Obviously, the player with slow reaction time will have fewer opportunities for success. Chapter 6, "Agility Training," and experience in gamelike conditions will teach players to make quick decisions and act on them with speed and coordination.

RUNNING MECHANICS

As mentioned before, every athlete can improve speed. It is simply a matter of commitment. Players must continue to work on developing strength and power but not at the expense of improving soccer skills. Therefore, coaches must alter the training schedule to avoid fatiguing athletes with negative side effects during practice sessions or matches.

In the general application of creating and maintaining speed, we will talk about the key elements that soccer athletes must work on. Although we will not attack the complicated technical track-and-field approach to running, the components of that method are fundamental to speed in any sport.

Stride Frequency

The term used to define the turnover of the legs is *frequency,* the speed at which the feet make contact with the ground over a given period. Assuming that the length of the stride is optimal, the more often the feet contact the ground, the more linear propulsion occurs and the faster the athlete will be. The athlete will move only if his feet are pushing the ground to the rear. The more times his feet push, the more speed he produces.

Strength and endurance allow an athlete to create and maintain speed. Plyometrics and strength training are the tools that make it possible for the legs to perform rapid and ballistic movements.

Stride Length

Although running style affects stride length, leg strength is a more important influence. Greater strength in the legs allows the stride to cover a longer distance, not by reaching out with the front leg but by pushing off the back foot. For example, if over 20 strides the athlete increases the distance by just three inches per stride, the distance covered will be five feet greater. In other words, an increase in stride length will result in greater speed if stride frequency remains the same.

Increasing stride length is necessary to increase speed, but this must not occur at the expense of good form. In attempting a longer stride, athletes tend to reach out with their lead leg, usually foot first instead of lifting at the knee. Although stride length may increase, two problems arise. First, while reaching out, the lead foot is in the air longer and is not in contact with the ground, which means that no pushing off occurs. Stride frequency, therefore, decreases. Remember, to increase speed, stride length and stride frequency cannot be sacrificed for one another. Second, because the leg is out in front of the body when the foot lands, a reduction of speed occurs. The greater the extension of the foot, the more resistance the body must overcome when the foot hits the ground.

Running Economy

Technically, the topic of running economy is complicated. A full discussion is outside the scope of this book. But through observing soccer athletes and other nontrack athletes, we conclude that increasing speed depends mostly on developing running economy.

The previously mentioned components, stride length and stride frequency, are essential to increasing speed. Although these components are crucial, they would be irrelevant if an athlete could not run correctly or efficiently in the first place.

A personal speed coach would be able to identify technical running errors, either by analyzing videotape or by seeing an athlete run in person. Even the greatest track athletes receive technical advice almost daily. For our purposes, the coach and athlete can learn to correct certain significant running flaws that will decidedly enhance the athlete's running speed in all directions.

Arm Carry

Observation of soccer athletes tells us that position and movement of the arms while running are issues. Players seldom use their arms effectively while running, and we know that an absence of arm swing detracts from the ability to reach top speed. When an athlete uses correct form, his arms seem to lead his body in powerful movement, whether it be running, jumping, or changing direction. In short, the arms lead the legs.

A good start for the proper position of the arm carry during a run is to begin with the arms at the sides and flexed at 90 degrees. The player should learn to swing her arms at the shoulder joints. The swing should be pendulum-like with a 90-degree flexion at the elbow joint. When her arm swings to the front, the athlete should not bring her hand past chest height. The backswing should go no farther than the back pocket. Arm movement should synchronize with leg movement, including forward movement in the form of marching. The athlete should begin with marching in place to learn the tempo of moving her arms and legs together. When the athlete is comfortable, forward movement can begin. The distance can be broken down into 20-yard (18-meter) segments for learning purposes.

Direction of the arm swing can also be critical. Crossing his arms over his midline (the imaginary line down the center of the trunk from nose to navel) can significantly alter mechanics and cost the athlete valuable time. Economy tells us that energy must go in the direction of the goal. Crossing the arms sends energy in a lateral direction.

Finally, excessive upward or downward motion can hinder speed production. An upward drive of the arms in a chariots-of-fire style of running produces too much vertical energy and can cause the entire body to lean back. Aggressive downward extension of the arms puts energy straight into the ground but, more important, keeps the legs from fully extending and altogether cuts off full movement.

Knee Lift

We know that running in any direction is a horizontal movement. Excessive knee lift goes against this notion. Besides putting too much vertical effort into the run, excessive knee lift causes two other problems. First, a high knee lift is accommodated by a backward lean of the body. Second, due in part to a backward lean, the stride is shortened. Although knee lift is important, excessive knee lift hinders speed.

Technical running errors can waste valuable energy, making players work harder than necessary. Developing running economy allows the athlete to get faster with less effort. So it's important that coaches and athletes invest the time into improving running form if needed, as it can pay off in huge dividends on the soccer field.

CHAPTER 8

INDIVIDUAL CONDITIONING DRILLS

Players can do many warm-up

exercises on an individual basis. In this way they learn how to do things on their own and at the same time improve their skills and fitness. You can start a training session with some of these exercises. Players should perform them at a slow tempo until they are warmed up. Stretching should also be included. We recommend that players run and stretch before they start these individual conditioning drills with a ball.

The drills in this chapter involve one ball per player. It is important in these drills to have already dealt with the player's running form. Soccer running involves sprinting from a walking start, sprinting from a jogging start, sprinting from a change of direction, and others kinds of movement. In addition, the patterns of walking, jogging, turning, and sprinting are varied. Therefore, these exercises should incorporate varied options to simulate the game.

DOUBLE-BOX EXERCISE

The small box is 15 by 20 yards (14 by 18 meters), and the big box is 30 by 40 yards (27 by 37 meters). Eight players, each with a ball, dribble while jogging in the smaller box. On the coach's command they dribble with the ball at top speed into the larger box and resume dribbling at a jog (as X_1 does in the diagram). On the next command they again sprint at top speed and return to the smaller box. At all times they avoid running into each other and try to dribble at speed into an open space. The coach can increase the demand of the exercise by requiring a particular feint (dribbling move) before the sprint. Some examples follow:

   a. Chop the ball with the inside of the foot, then sprint.
   b. Chop the ball with the outside of the foot, then sprint.
   c. Chop the ball behind the standing leg, then sprint.
   d. Perform a scissors move, then sprint.
   e. Perform a stepover move, then sprint.
   f. Perform a spin turn, then sprint.

Use your imagination to come up with other feints for your players to perform. You can also alter the start position by having the players walk with the ball and then sprint on your command. The fitness component emphasizes short-distance power and speed, so besides working on technique, your players perform repetitive short sprints.

WALL KICKS

A wall can be a best friend to a coach or a player. A wall is a good place for players to work on quickness and reactions from a physical and technical standpoint. A player can kick the ball against the wall and as it rebounds, quickly adjust body position to trap the ball, prepare it, and kick again. Restrictions increase the demands. For example, a player can

a. use only inside-of-the-foot passing,

b. use only the instep,

c. alternate between the left foot and right foot with any technique,

d. restrict touches to two or even one, or

e. move closer to the wall, lift the ball in the air against the wall, and allow only one bounce before kicking again.

These drill variations and others that you create can increase your players' ability to react quickly and efficiently to the ball.

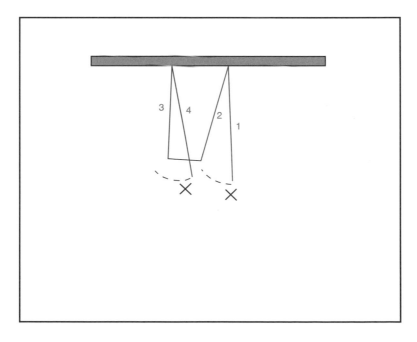

PLAYER/BALL SPRINT OR RACE

Each player starts at the midfield line and jogs while dribbling the ball toward the penalty box. After reaching the penalty box, the player pushes the ball firmly forward and sprints after it, trying to trap the ball on the end line of the field. The player then turns and dribbles back to midfield at a jog to repeat the exercise.

This exercise works on sprinting and builds aerobic fitness by including a jog of 85 to 100 yards (78 to 91 meters) before every sprint. Players should repeat the drill as appropriate to age and fitness work desired.

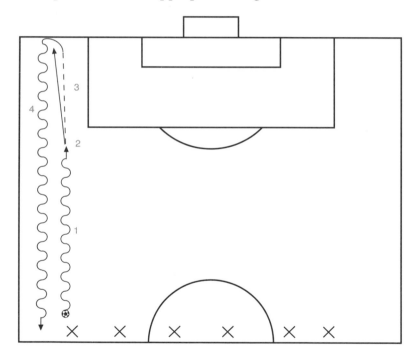

REACTION LATERAL SPRINT WITH BALL ACTIVITY

The player has the ball at her feet and is between two cones that are 15 to 20 yards (14 to 18 meters) apart. She could be resting or performing a light activity (for example, tapping the ball alternately with her left and right foot). On the coach's command, she sprints to the cone indicated and back to the middle. The player then resumes the initial activity. She must react and sprint off in a lateral direction. Not all soccer running is straight ahead. The ability to turn and quickly reach top speed is vital. The coach can add cones in front of and behind the player to enhance this drill and can require a feint before the sprint.

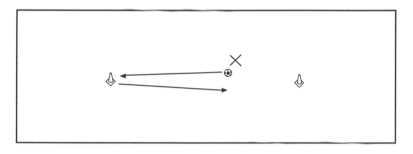

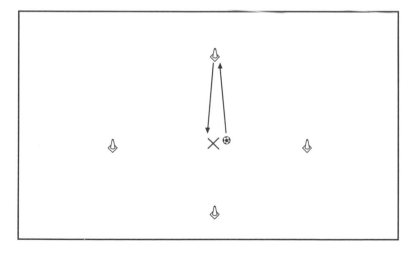

FITNESS SHOOTING

Shooting exercises for players can also incorporate fitness. In games players often get into a shooting position after sprinting and are in a fatigued state. So good game preparation includes shooting when tired or after a sprint.

The coach has the soccer balls. A player sprints back and forth between two flags that are five to seven yards apart and parallel to the goal. On the coach's signal the coach passes the ball forward, and the player sprints after it to shoot on goal. Various restrictions can be applied. For example, the player may be required to

a. sprint back and forth,

b. alternately sprint and backpedal,

c. jump and perform an imaginary header after reaching each flag, or

d. perform lateral side-shuffling movements between flags.

This exercise can be set up in different areas of the field around the penalty box to alter the angle of the shots.

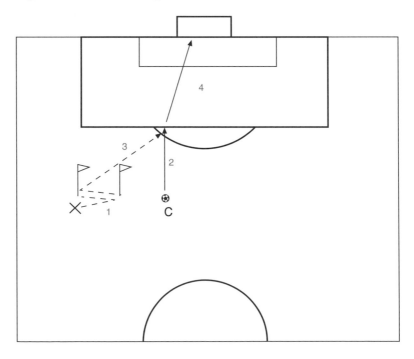

STATIONARY JUGGLE-TRAP-SPRINT

In a random space each player juggles a ball and at a distance of 10 yards (9 meters) or so from the nearest player. After three or four juggles the player kicks the ball slightly higher into the air. As the ball comes down she traps the ball into space and immediately sprints with the ball for 10 to 15 yards (9 to 14 meters). The player then repeats the exercise. A number of different traps can be used—inside of the foot, outside of the foot, instep, chest, thigh, and others. The coach can require that players do perhaps five of each trap. The fitness element is the repetitive sprinting and the change of direction that should result from trapping the ball.

MOVING JUGGLE-TRAP-SPRINT

The player starts at the midfield line and juggles the ball while moving toward the penalty box. After reaching the penalty box he traps the ball, turns, sprints back to the midfield line, and then repeats the exercise.

For better players the juggling part of this exercise provides rest, which should allow complete recovery before each sprint. Depending on field size the sprint will be between 35 and 40 yards (32 to 37 meters). The coach can specify how to juggle and what kind of trap to use.

Many other exercises are available. We offer here several drills that incorporate skill work with fitness. The exercises are generally set up to provide interval training, which builds fitness relevant to soccer. Whenever you can simulate game conditions in your training sessions, you enhance the progress of your team.

CHAPTER 9

TEAM CONDITIONING DRILLS

Exercises that train players

in groups of two or three are efficient because the interval method is inherent; one partner works while the others rests. This method can be more enjoyable because motivated players push each other to better performances. Finally, partner drills establish the initial team building block of working in pairs.

TEAM DRILL 1

Create a grid size appropriate to the age of your players (pitches vary in size but average about 120 by 60 yards [110 by 55 meters]) and pair them up. If you have a team of 16 high-school-age players, use half the soccer field as your working area.

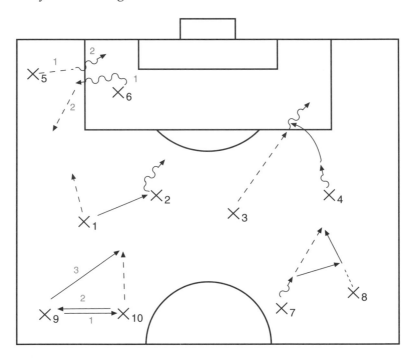

Players jog and pass the ball in this area while constantly maintaining movement. Every two or three minutes, depending on fatigue, players rest and stretch for one to one and a half minutes. Within each work period the coach can make various demands on the players:

• After passing to player 2, player 1 should sprint for 10 to 15 yards (9 to 14 meters). Besides developing fitness, the player learns to move after passing the ball.

• Player 3 sprints into an open space to receive a leading pass from player 4. The sprint should be at least 20 yards (18 meters). Players learn to make the run in advance of the pass. Timing is important. Player 4 must be ready to play the ball to player 3, and player 3's sprint must not be too early or too late.

• Player 6 dribbles away from player 5 and then dribbles toward player 5, who runs toward the player 6 to execute a takeover move. Both players sprint away after exchanging the ball, and they repeat the move 10 to 15 seconds later. In this variation players learn to combine with each other and sprint after playing the ball.

• While dribbling, player 7 looks for player 8. The player then passes the ball to player 8 and sprints to an open space to collect the return pass, called a wall pass. Player 8 returning the pass to the sprinting player can play with either one or two touches. Again, players learn to combine.

• Player 9 plays a pass to a partner, player 10, who plays the ball immediately back to player 9. After playing the pass, player 10 sprints into an open space and receives a return pass from player 9. This two-player combination is known as a double pass.

In this exercise, players learn two-player combinations and receive fitness and speed training. The sprinting occurs at intervals relevant to soccer, after making a pass and before collecting a pass. All pairs perform the same variation for a two- or three-minute period. After a rest break they can repeat the variation or do another. Remember that for your players to perform quality sprints and execution, they must work in intervals.

TEAM DRILL 2

A two-player combination running to goal with shooting can also be used for speed work. Two examples follow.

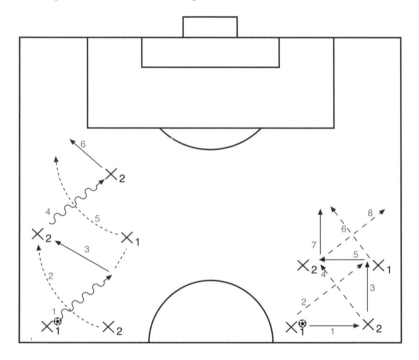

• For an overlapping combination, player 1 dribbles in at a diagonal as player 2 makes a bending run behind the run of player 1. Player 1 then plays the pass and starts to make an overlapping run. The player receiving the first pass runs in a diagonal to set up the second overlap.

• Player 1 plays a square pass to player 2. Immediately after making the pass, player 1 sprints forward in a diagonal path to receive a forward pass from player 2. Player 2 then runs diagonally to the other side to receive a square pass from player 1 to repeat the pattern.

Finishing either pattern with a shot on goal is optional. Again, timing of the runs is important, and players should perform quality sprinting bursts.

TEAM DRILL 3

This two-player fitness routine incorporates the ball and is an anaerobic activity that uses a work period, a rest period, and a period of light activity. The rest-to-work interval is 2:1. For younger players the duration of each period should be 30 seconds; for players of high-school age and older, 45 seconds is ideal.

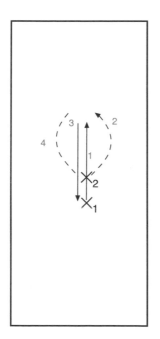 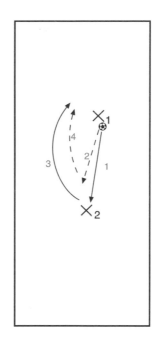

- Player 1 has the ball at the feet. Player 2 is one yard away with feet spread and facing the player with the ball. Player 1 pushes a pass through player 2's legs. The second player turns and sprints to retrieve the ball, passes it back to player 1, and returns to the starting position as quickly as possible. Players repeat this sequence for the entire work period. The player passing the ball should try to play it 10 yards (9 meters).

- Player 1, with the ball, stands 10 yards from player 2. Player 1 passes the ball to player 2 and follows the pass. Player 2 then chips the ball over player 1's head. Player 1 quickly turns and tries to trap the ball, allowing as few bounces as possible. If players cannot chip the ball with their feet, have them collect the pass with their hands and throw it over the partner's head.

In the previous drills one player rests while the other works. The light-activity period takes place after both have worked. Examples of light activity are one-touch passing back and forth, juggling the ball with each other, or heading the ball back and forth.

- In this drill players sprint and exchange passes. The players start 20 yards (18 meters) apart. At the start command they sprint to exchange positions. One player sprints with a ball; the other sprints without it. When they have exchanged positions, the player with the ball passes to the partner, and they repeat the drill. They keep going until the work period has expired.

- In this drill players exchange the ball in the middle. The setup is the same as the one used in the previous drill. Player 1 dribbles the ball, and player 2 sprints without the ball. Halfway across the 20-yard channel, player 1 leaves the ball for player 2 (the takeover) and continues sprinting without the ball. Player 2 continues with the ball. When they arrive at opposite sides, they turn and repeat the activity until the work period is over.

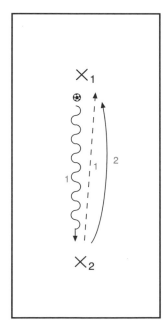
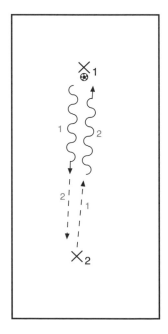

In the two previous drills, both players work at the same time. Therefore, they have the same rest period and perform a light-activity period as described earlier. The unillustrated drills below are two more drills that rotate resting and working players.

- To start the sit-up headers drill, player 1 is on his or her back in a preparatory sit-up position. Player 2 has the ball and stands in front of player 1's feet. Every time player 1 does a sit-up, player 2 serves the ball so that player 1 can head it back at the apex of the sit-up.

- To practice jumping and diving headers, the players stand about five yards apart with the resting player holding the ball. The player with the ball throws the ball up so that the working player must jump to head it back. Immediately after getting the ball back, the first player serves a low ball that the working player can head back only by diving forward and landing on the hands and body. The resting player then serves the ball in the air to repeat the sequence.

These last two drills are designed to develop strength and power. If you are using all six drills in your fitness sessions, sequence them so that the heading exercises are separated by two running exercises.

TEAM DRILL 4

Circuit training is a good example of fitness training for soccer. Circuit training can be done with or without the ball. The example that follows is done in pairs and incorporates the ball. The circuit incorporates a 45-second to 60-second work period, an equal rest period, and a similar period to move on to the next station. The stations are designed to work different aspects of fitness, with every third work station easier to allow full intensity on the others. The following is an example of the many possible options:

- Station 1: Two players juggle back and forth for the duration of both work periods.
- Station 2: Players perform sit-up headers as described earlier.
- Station 3: Starting at the six-yard-box line, one player sprints to the top of the D outside the penalty box and back to the six-yard box. At this point the partner serves a ball for the player to volley into the net. Players then repeat the exercise.
- Station 4: One player serves the ball to the other with the hands. The working player traps the ball with the thigh or chest and returns the ball with an inside-of-the-foot pass.
- Station 5: While standing, the player throws (if skills are good enough the player can kick it) the ball in the air, quickly sits down, gets up, and traps the ball with the feet as the ball hits the ground. The player repeats the sequence for the entire work period.
- Station 6: The player starts on the goal line in front of the goal. He or she sprints to the 6-yard line (goal box) and back and then sprints to the 18-yard line (penalty box) and back, receiving on the way back a lob from the partner to head into the goal. The player repeats the exercise.

If you have portable goals set the shooting stations on some other part of the field. In the diagram we have used a soccer field. Players can start at any station, but they must rotate in an organized manner. A clockwise or counterclockwise rotation is easiest. The sample circuit, which covers sprinting, abdominal work, and technique, trains the anaerobic system and uses interval-training principles.

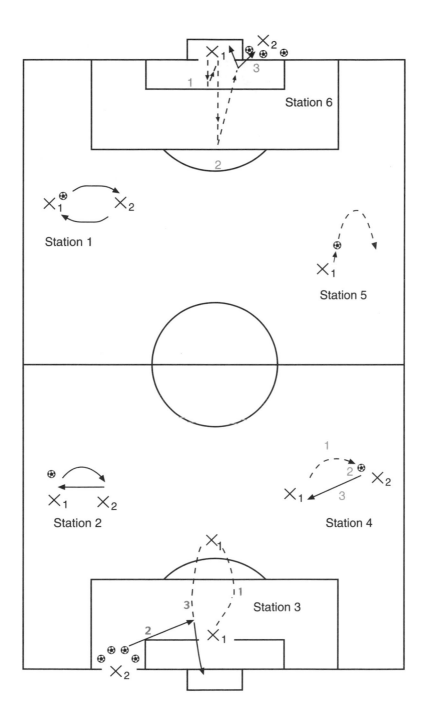

Station 6

Station 1

Station 5

Station 2

Station 4

Station 3

TEAM DRILL 5

Two players work together with one ball. They start at one sideline, standing level with each other about 10 yards (9 meters) apart. On the coach's signal they start to sprint toward the other side of the field while passing the ball back and forth between them. After reaching the other side they turn and sprint back. For high-school-age players the object is to complete 2 legs, or 160 yards (146 meters), in 30 seconds. After working for 30 seconds they rest for 30 seconds and then have a light activity period for 30 seconds. Repetitions should not exceed 10 and should start at 5 the first time you try this with your team.

This anaerobic-fitness routine is best done at the end of practice.

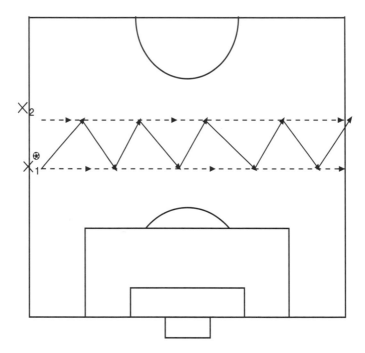

TEAM DRILL 6

Exercises can also be done in groups of three. The following can serve as a warm-up that leads into quickness and speed work, or you can drop some of the early progressions and use the exercise for fitness training during the middle or at the end of practice.

The players are in groups of three, so we have a rest-to-work ratio of 2:1. Two players, one with a ball, face the third. The distance between the players is 20 yards (18 meters). The player with the ball dribbles to the other side and gives the ball to the player there, who returns with the ball and gives it to next player. To use this as a warm-up, players begin with these activities:

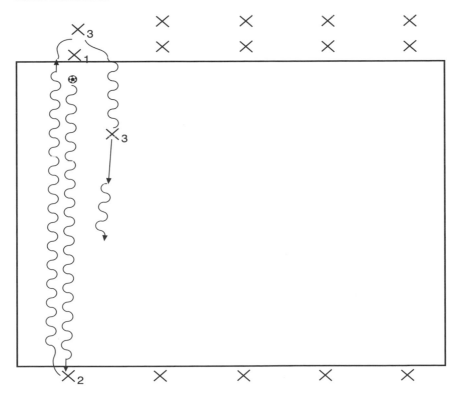

a. Dribble across at 50 percent speed.

b. Dribble across by touching the ball with the inside of the feet, alternating between the left and right foot with each step.

c. Run sideways and drag the ball with the sole of the right foot. Use the sole of the left foot the next time.

d. Go backward and drag the ball by using the sole of the feet, alternating between the right and left foot with each step.

e. Go forward and drag the ball by using the sole of the feet, alternating between the right and left foot with each step.

f. Dribble across at 75 percent speed.

Now we are ready to perform some turning, sprinting, and skill work. In this phase each player makes two feints or turns in the middle of the area. The first turn has the player going back to where he or she started, and the second has the player going to the other side again.

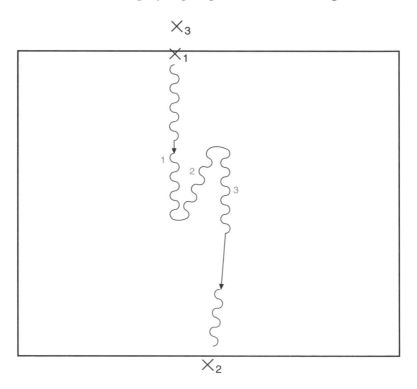

g. Chop the ball with the inside of the foot to turn.

h. Chop the ball with the outside of the foot to turn.

i. Chop the ball behind the standing leg to turn.

j. Step over and turn using the inside or outside of the foot.

In performing turns g through j, players must concentrate on quickness in the turns and explode into and out of every turn. They do each move for two minutes and then move onto the next one. The players get a short break between moves while you explain the next move. These suggestions are just a few examples of the feints you can use.

SMALL-GROUP GAMES FOR 3 TO 11 PLAYERS

Many small-group games in soccer are played at the beginning of practice. These games are a good activity because they incorporate technique and tactical understanding of the game. There are also ways to get a little extra fitness out of these active warm-up games.

We begin with traditional possession-type games used in soccer. In these games the main object is for a team to keep possession of the ball as long as possible.

5-V-2 KEEP-AWAY

In this game you should apply a limitation on touches for each player. The better the skills of the player, the fewer touches you should allow, to as few as one. Add the aerobic fitness element by requiring the whole group to move to where the ball landed after a bad pass. This provision eliminates standing around and keeps the players mentally alert.

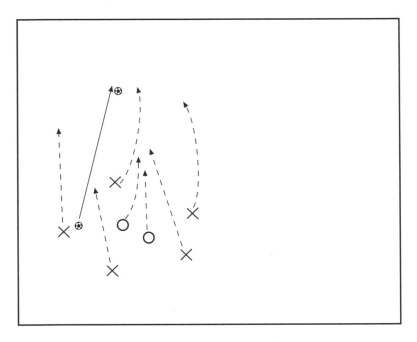

   The game continues after the group moves to the ball. The player who was in the middle for the longest time joins the outside players. The player who made the bad pass goes into the middle.

4-V-2 KEEP-AWAY

The principles of this game are the same as those in 5-v-2. In this game, however, the lowest touch restriction for your skilled players would be two touches. The fitness element is added by requiring the two defenders accumulate three points to get out of the middle. In this way the defensive pair works for a longer period and earns a reward for intense and smart defensive play.

The defensive pair earns a point if they force an errant pass, intercept the ball, or radically change the ball's direction and kick the ball out of the grid. They lose a point if the four attackers complete a pass that goes between the two defenders or if the attackers play a ball through a defender's legs and complete a pass. A scoring option is for the defenders to lose a point if the attackers complete a string of passes, numbering perhaps 15 for skilled players.

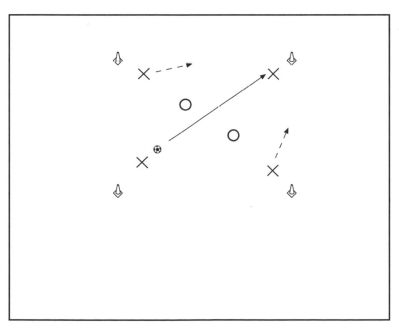

The grid for high-school-age players should be 15 yards (14 meters) square. Adjust the size to your team's age and skill level. Players enjoy this game because it is competitive. The defenders need to work hard (fitness element) and smart (tactical element). After the defending pair earns three points, another pair goes in. Continue this rotation until all three pairs have been in the middle.

6-V-3 KEEP-AWAY, THREE-TEAM GAME

The previous four games involve changing the player or players in the middle at a certain point. The games must stop briefly while the players change roles. This game requires changes to be made as the game continues.

Divide nine players into three groups of three. Each group wears a training bib of a different color, say, white, red, and blue. Suppose that the blues start in the middle. The six players in white and red try to keep the ball away from the blue team. If the blue team intercepts the ball or the red or white team kicks the ball out of bounds, the blues no longer defend. The team that kicked the ball out or had it intercepted would go in the middle, and the blues and whites would try to keep the ball away from them.

Use a minimum grid size of 20 by 30 yards (18 by 27 meters) for skilled players, and play with a two-touch restriction for the six. Adjust size and touch for your players' age and skill level. Play should continue for three to four minutes before players have a break.

This game requires constant motion. Even after turnovers the game continues without a break. Players must perform both physically and mentally. They need to be sharp.

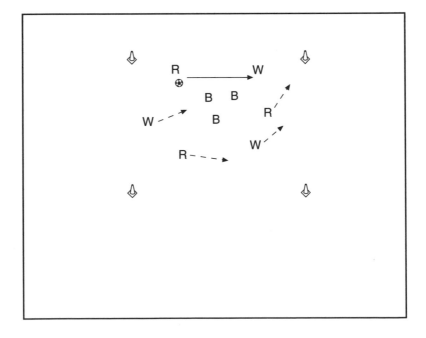

7-V-4 KEEP-AWAY

This game has a different wrinkle. (It can also be played 8-v-4, but you should have at least three more attackers than you have defenders.) In this possession game the defenders work as a group until they get six points. The grid should be at least 25 by 30 yards (23 by 27 meters), but it can be larger to require players to run more.

When the four defenders win possession of the ball, they score two points if they can successfully dribble the ball out of the grid. The attackers must immediately become defenders to prevent the four from getting outside the grid. Because they have extra players, they should be able to double-team the player with the ball.

The four defenders score one point if they force a bad pass that goes out of bounds. This game requires instant transition, as in a real soccer match, and players must react quickly and efficiently to the turnover. The defenders must work hard, which tests their anaerobic fitness, because they are playing with fewer players. After gaining possession they must become offensive players to score points.

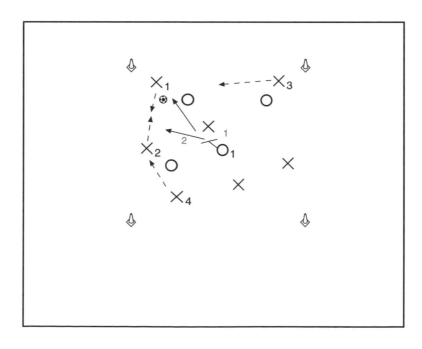

TRANSITION SHOOTING GAME

All the preceding small-group games are possession games. This small-group game incorporates finishing and shooting. The size of the area should be 40 by 45 yards (37 by 41 meters), although it can be longer if you want to increase fitness demands. The field should include two regular-size goals with goalkeepers.

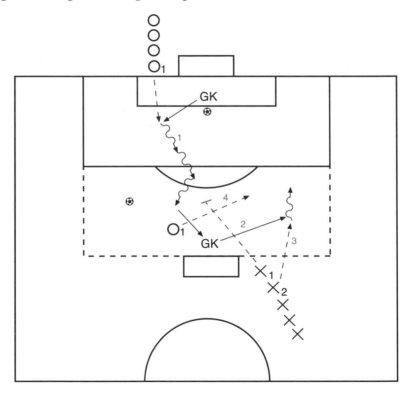

Line up two groups of five players outside the goal posts at opposite sides of the smaller field as shown in the diagram. O_1 starts the play after receiving a pass from his goalkeeper. He then goes 1v1 against X_1 with O_1 trying to get a shot on goal. After this shot the other goalkeeper distributes the saved ball or a new ball to X_2 who goes against O_1, who becomes a defender. X_2 attempts a shot on goal against O_1. The first goalkeeper distributes the ball to O_2 to face another X defender. There is a constant flow to the game allowing shooting, defending and good practice for goalkeepers.

3-V-2 KEEP-AWAY

For this possession game the grid should be at least 15 by 20 yards (14 by 18 meters). When the defenders intercept the ball or a bad pass goes out of the grid, the defender who was in the longest joins the three attackers. The player who committed the turnover joins the middle. The touch limitation for skilled players should be three touches. All others should play unlimited touch.

The small number of players should create high intensity. Therefore, the game should be played interval style. Players should play for two to three minutes and then have a break of one to two minutes. To increase the fitness demands of the game, simply make the grid larger. This game combines technique, tactics, and anaerobic-fitness training.

2-V-1 KEEP-AWAY

Players cannot hide in this possession game. The defender is all alone, and when one of the attackers has the ball the other one must move because there is no one else. Play this game interval style with one-minute work periods in a grid no larger than 20 yards (18 meters) square. During rest periods players should perform a light activity like juggling in threes, one-touch passing, or heading back and forth.

This game is great for promoting movement off the ball and increasing the fitness level of your players.

4-V-4+2 KEEP-AWAY GAME

In this possession game we introduce the concept of jokers. The jokers, in this game the two additional players, are always part of the team that possesses the ball. The result is a 6-v-4 game. The grid size is ideally 25 by 40 yards (23 by 37 meters). Start with unlimited touch but reduce to two-touch or even one-touch for skilled players.

Reducing the number of touches increases player movement. The two jokers must work constantly to get open for the team in possession because they are the extra players. Play this game in four- or five-minute intervals with a one- to two-minute break. Change the jokers with each interval. For increased fitness make the grid larger; the four defenders will really have to work. To increase the demand on quickness, make the grid a little smaller. This game combines all the components of soccer and is great for developing soccer fitness.

CHAPTER 10

PROGRAM DESIGN

Now that we have covered

all the components of a training program, it is time to put them into a yearlong program. Coaches often know the elements of a training program but have trouble meshing the ingredients into a balanced year-round approach. Every component affects the others, so it is critical to schedule components in the appropriate time of year and understand the overall effect of the various combinations.

The following off-season, preseason, and in-season schedules illustrate how to combine the components—warm-up and flexibility, speed improvement, plyometrics, agility, conditioning, and weight training—on a weekly basis.

The schedules are examples of effective weekly workouts or practices. Every athlete or team has a unique situation. By understanding the philosophy of scheduling each training component, the coach can design a schedule for any scenario.

OFF-SEASON TRAINING

We present here a sample 12-week program for soccer players during the off-season. The off-season could be up to 32 weeks long. During the off-season, players work on building overall strength, improving cardiovascular fitness, and sharpening speed and agility. Plyometrics and agility drills are absent in the early weeks, appearing in the schedule only after the athlete has established an appropriate base of strength and fitness.

Use this as a guideline to design a systematic conditioning program specific to your team's needs.

OFF-SEASON

Weeks 1-4

Monday

Warm-up and flexibility

Speed improvement—50-yard (46-meter) jogs × 10–15, working on arm carry, knee lift, and body lean

Conditioning—20- to 30-minute run at 150 bpm

Weight training—Incline press 3 × 12; military press 3 × 12; lat pull-down 3 × 12; seated row 3 × 12; barbell curl 3 × 12; and lying triceps extension 3 × 12

Tuesday

Warm-up and flexibility

Speed improvement—50-yard (46-meter) jogs × 10–15, working on arm carry, knee lift, and body lean

Conditioning—Lifecycle: level 3 at 90 rpm for 5 minutes, levels 7 to 10 at 90 rpm for 20 to 30 minutes

Weight training—Clean deadlifts 3 × 12; leg press 5 × 12; leg extension 2 × 20; leg curl 4 × 12; hyperextension, body weight 3 × 15; and seated calf 3 × 15

Wednesday

No training

Thursday

Warm-up and flexibility

Speed improvement—50-yard (46-meter) jogs × 10–15, working on arm carry, knee lift, and body lean

Conditioning—20- to 30-minute run at 150 bpm

Weight training—Incline press 3 × 12; military press 3 × 12; lat pulldown 3 × 12; seated row 3 × 12; barbell curl 3 × 12; and lying triceps extension 3 × 12

Friday

Warm-up and flexibility

Speed improvement—50-yard (46-meter) jogs × 10–15, working on arm carry, knee lift, and body lean

Conditioning—Lifecycle: level 3 at 90 rpm for 5 minutes, levels 7 to 10 at 90 rpm for 20 to 30 minutes

Weight training—Clean deadlift 3 × 12; leg press 5 × 12; leg extension 2 × 20; leg curl 4 × 12; hyperextension, body weight 3 × 15; and seated calf 3 × 15

Saturday

No training

Sunday

No training

Summary

Warm-Up and Flexibility

Whenever the training program includes movement—conditioning, agility training, plyometrics, light jogging—the warm-up and flexibility segment will involve both stretching and running warm-up. This portion of the training day remains unchanged until the preseason and in-season program, when touching the ball becomes part of the warm-up.

Speed Improvement

Because running mechanics are best taught at slow speeds first and at faster speeds later, it makes sense to include low-intensity running during the early stages of training in the off-season. This low-intensity running helps lay the foundation for early fitness.

Plyometrics

During this early part of the training program, athletes do not perform plyometrics because they lack strength and fitness. Performing plyometrics too early in the training cycle could lead to poor training results and possible injury.

Agility

Like plyometrics, agility training is best done after athletes have acquired enough strength and fitness to perform the drills correctly (speed, reaction time).

Conditioning

Low-intensity cardiovascular training begins the off-season training cycle. To develop a better fitness base, athletes do a higher volume (20 to 40 minutes) than they do during the rest of the year. Running is not an important part of conditioning early in the training year. The remainder of the year will offer adequate opportunity to run. Running too much too soon at high intensity can lead to burnout, overtraining, and injury. Athletes should use low-impact cardio machines such as Lifecycle, Stairmaster, or elliptical trainers. The focus is to prepare the heart and lungs for higher intensity later in the year.

Weight Training

The main objective in the beginning is general preparation. Athletes perform basic exercises that target the whole body and use many repetitions at low intensity (light weights). Technique is easier to learn with low-intensity loads, and performing many repetitions will allow athletes to gain weight-training fitness for heavier loads later in the training cycle. The format shown is a four-day split that works both the upper and lower body twice per week. This schedule is effective for off-season weight training.

OFF-SEASON

Weeks 5–8

Monday

Warm-up and flexibility

Agility—Four-corners drill: 2 × 3, 5 yards (5 meters); forward and backward: 2 × 10, 10 yards (9 meters); and lateral shuffle: 2 × 10, 15 yards (14 meters)

Weight training—Incline press 3 × 8; military press 3 × 8; lat pulldown 4 × 8; seated row 4 × 8; barbell curl 3 × 8; and lying triceps extension 4 × 8

Conditioning—Stride 10 × 80 yards (73 meters) with 21-second intervals, two-minute rest; 10 × 40 yards (37 meters) with 9-second intervals, two-minute rest; and 10 × 20 yards (18 meters) with 6-second rest

Tuesday

Warm-up and flexibility

Plyometrics—Side to side: 2 × 10, 6 inches (15 centimeters); max vertical jump: 3 × 5; and standing long jump: 3 × 5

Weight training—Clean pull 5 × 5; leg press 4 × 8; leg extension 3 × 20; leg curl 5 × 8; hyperextension, 25 pounds (11 kilograms), 4 × 8; and seated calf 2 × 15

Wednesday

Warm-up and flexibility

Conditioning—20-minute jog

Thursday

Warm-up and flexibility

Agility—Four-corners drill: 2 × 3, 5 yards (5 meters); forward and backward: 2 × 10, 10 yards (9 meters); and lateral shuffle: 2 × 10, 15 yards (14 meters)

Weight training—Incline press 3 × 8; military press 3 × 8; lat pulldown 4 × 8; seated row 4 × 8; barbell curl 3 × 8; and lying triceps extension 4 × 8

Conditioning—Stride 10 × 80 yards (73 meters) with 21-second intervals, two-minute rest; 10 × 40 yards (37 meters) with 9-second intervals, two-minute rest; and 10 × 20 yards (18 meters) with 6-second rest

Friday

Warm-up and flexibility

Plyometrics—Side to side: 2 × 10, 6 inches (15 centimeters); max vertical jump: 3 × 5; and standing long jump: 3 × 5

Weight training—Clean pull 5 × 5; leg press 4 × 8; leg extension 3 × 20; leg curl 5 × 8; hyperextension, 25 pounds (11 kilograms), 4 × 8; and seated calf 2 × 15

Saturday

No training

Sunday

No training

Summary

Warm-Up and Flexibility

As stated earlier, this part of the program will have only subtle changes throughout the year. During this part of the training, because of the addition of agility drills, the coach may want to include more lateral and angular movements. Short hopping and hip flexion and extension should be added on the plyometric days.

Speed Improvement

During the warm-up jog before conditioning, players can practice running mechanics. This excellent warm-up can be continued as athletes increase speed in an effort to reach conditioning speed.

Plyometrics

Following weeks of conditioning and strengthening, athletes are ready for a low-level plyometric program. As illustrated here, the drills must be two-footed and basic. A well-rounded plyometric program includes work on the lateral, vertical, and horizontal planes.

Agility

Like the plyometric program, agility training begins with basic movement. Fundamental change-of-direction drills that do not require top speed or complex movements are the menu preference. At this point the goal is proper execution, not speed.

Conditioning

The intensity and yardage continue to progress as interval training is introduced. Athletes are not prepared to engage in 100 percent speed activities, so the next step after jogging is striding. In the initial phase of interval training a frequency of twice per week is preferable. With the increase in yardage and intensity, athletes need plenty of time between workouts to recover. In this example, Wednesday is a light jogging day, although the light day can be placed anywhere in the training week. Despite the increase in conditioning intensity, a need remains for additional yardage, and light jogging serves that purpose.

Weight Training

The necessary decrease in repetitions is illustrated with every exercise. A progression is also found with the clean deadlift, which now becomes the clean pull. The decrease in number of repetitions shows a move toward absolute strength. An increase in number of repetitions would indicate that the objective is endurance. In soccer, athletes build endurance through drilling, conditioning, and games. Weight training for soccer athletes emphasizes strength and power.

The repetition zone for the clean pulls begins at about five. For any other exercise, the repetition zone would be higher, but the clean pull requires a great deal of technique. Performing more repetitions of the clean pull with correct technique would be difficult. The repetition foundation is found in the less technical primary exercise, the clean deadlift.

OFF-SEASON

Weeks 9-12

Monday

Warm-up and flexibility

Agility—Four-corners drill: 2 × 5, 2 yards (2 meters); forward and backward: change of direction on cue, 15-second drills × 6; and lateral shuffle: 4 × 10, 5 yards (5 meters)

Weight training—Incline press 3 × 3; military press 3 × 5; lat pulldown 4 × 5; seated row 4 × 5; barbell curl 3 × 5; and lying triceps extension 4 × 5

Conditioning—Stride 6 × 100 yards (91 meters) with 27-second intervals, two-minute rest; 6 × 60 yards (55 meters) with 15-second intervals, two-minute rest; sprint 6 × 40 yards (37 meters) with 45-second rest intervals, four-minute rest; and 6 × 20 yards (18 meters) with 22-second rest interval

Tuesday

Warm-up and flexibility

Plyometrics—One-legged side to side: 2 × 10, 6 inches (15 centimeters); repeat triple max vertical jump: 5 × 3; and repeat triple standing long jump: 3 × 3

Weight training—Clean pull 5 × 2; leg press 5 × 3; leg extension 3 × 15; leg curl 6 × 5; hyperextension, 35 pounds (16 kilograms), 4 × 5; and seated calf 3 × 10

Wednesday

Warm-up and flexibility

Medium- to high-intensity soccer scrimmages

Thursday

Warm-up and flexibility

Agility—Figure 8: 10 repetitions at 5 yards (5 meters); forward and backward: change of direction on cue, 15-second drills × 6; and lateral shuffle: change of direction on cue, 15-second drills × 6

Weight training—Incline press 3 × 3; military press 3 × 5; lat pulldown 4 × 5; seated row 4 × 5; barbell curl 3 × 5; and lying triceps extension 4 × 5

Conditioning—Stride 6 × 100 yards (91 meters) with 27-second intervals, two-minute rest; 6 × 60 yards (55 meters) with 15-second intervals, two-minute rest; sprint 6 × 40 yards (37 meters) with 45-second rest intervals, four-minute rest; and 6 × 20 yards (18 meters) with 22-second rest interval

Friday

Warm-up and flexibility

Plyometrics—Angle hop: 10 × 15 yards (14 meters); repeat triple max vertical jump: 5 × 3; and repeat triple standing long jump: 3 × 3

Weight training—Clean pull 5 × 2; leg press 5 × 3; leg extension 3 × 15; leg curl 6 × 5; hyperextension, 35 pounds (16 kilograms), 4 × 5; and seated calf 3 × 10

Saturday

Warm-up and flexibility

Medium- to high-intensity soccer scrimmages

Sunday

Warm-up and flexibility

Medium-intensity soccer scrimmages

Optional: 20- to 30-minute aerobic activity, using bike, stepper, or other activity, but no running

Summary

Warm-Up and Flexibility

As in the midcycle, the warm-up should include more ballistic activities because of the presence of plyometrics, agility training, and sprinting.

Speed Improvement

Running mechanics should be monitored but not necessarily emphasized as part of the training. By now athletes should be running correctly at slow speeds out of habit. Running mechanics should be paid attention to during all runs that are not 100 percent speed or effort.

Plyometrics

The normal progression continues as more advanced drills are implemented, such as one-legged and multiple-response drills. The progression of the drills depends on the training level of the athlete and previous exposure to specific drills.

Agility

The key here is not to overdo the drilling. Athletes will start to play more scrimmages and pickup games, activities that require plenty of agility. Although the drills continue to advance to a higher level, the coach must avoid overtraining the players. To increase speed of movement, distances of some of the drills are reduced.

Conditioning

The yardage and intensity have increased to the point that sprinting can be added. In the example, sprinting has been added to the day of the stride interval workouts. If an athlete has a low level of work capacity, she should sprint on a day other than the stride day. Notice that players are now engaged in scrimmages of medium to high intensity. These matches can involve full sides or 3-v-3, 4-v-4, and so on. Because these matches work on the players' fitness, they need to perform conditioning only twice per week. When designing plyometrics, agility, and conditioning during the late cycle, the coach must recognize the duration and intensity of scrimmages during the week. Too much activity heightens the risk of overtraining and mental burnout.

Weight Training

It is no surprise here that the repetition range has dropped significantly, not only from the beginning of the off-season but from the midseason as well. A lowered repetition range during this time of year serves two purposes. First, it focuses on promoting strength, and second, it reduces the amount of fatigue so that athletes can increase their work level in conditioning and scrimmages.

PRESEASON TRAINING

Daily practice sessions mark the preseason training program. Whereas the off-season program is geared primarily toward total conditioning, the major objective during the preseason is to raise the physical readiness of athletes for the upcoming season, improve skills, and develop strategies. Because practicing soccer and improving game fitness are the focus, time spent on training outside the game decreases. The preseason is usually two to four weeks long.

PRESEASON

Weeks 1–4

Monday

Conditioning—Stride 6 × 100 yards (91 meters) with 24-second rest; 6 × 80 yards (73 meters) with 18-second rest; and 6 × 60 yards (55 meters) with 12-second rest

Weight training—Incline press 3 × 5 and military press 3 × 5, 30- to 45-second rest between sets

Tuesday

Plyometrics—Repeat tuck jump: 3–5 sets × 5 repetitions and single-leg hop 2–3 sets × 5, 10 yards (9 meters)

Conditioning—Sprint 20 × 20 yards (18 meters), 20- to 30-second rest

Weight training—Lat pulldown 4 × 5 and seated row 4 × 5, 30- to 45-second rest between sets

Wednesday

Conditioning—10- to 15-minute light recovery jog

Weight training—Clean pull 3 × 3; leg press 3 × 3; and leg curl 4 × 5, 30- to 45-second rest between sets

Thursday

Conditioning—Stride 4 × 50 yards (46 meters) with 10-second rest; 4 × 40 yards (37 meters) with 10-second rest; 4 × 30 yards (27 meters) with 10-second rest; 4 × 20 yards (18 meters) with 5-second rest; and 4 × 10 yards (9 meters) with 5-second rest

Weight training—Barbell curl 3 × 5 and lying triceps extension 4 × 5, 30- to 45-second rest between sets

Friday

Plyometrics—Max vertical jump 3–5 sets × 5 repetitions, single

Conditioning—None because of practice game the following day

Weight training—Makeup day for any missed days during the week

Saturday

Practice game

Weight training—Makeup day for any missed days during the week

Sunday

Easy practice session to prepare for the beginning of heavy training on
   Monday—no plyometrics, weight training, or conditioning

Summary

Warm-Up and Flexibility

The daily warm-up begins with the practice session and is extensive
and soccer specific. Agility training, plyometrics, and conditioning are
included in the daily practice schedule, so there is no need to have
another warm-up session other than the prepractice activity. All weight
training follows the practice session. Soccer practice for the day will be
more than enough to prepare the athlete for weight training immediately following.

Agility

Drilling with the ball is the best form of agility training during the
preseason period. Any use of agility drills should be basic and in a
warm-up format. An obstacle course or pattern drill using the ball works
well. Drills should focus on movement and coordination with the ball.
Because these drills require precision, players should perform them at
the beginning of practice before fatigue sets in.

Plyometrics

Lower-body plyometrics are the dominant drills for soccer athletes, and
during this period of training, leg fatigue will be the greatest. Therefore,
the plyometric menu should be basic and low volume, performed once
or twice per week.

Conditioning

When determining the volume of conditioning you must consider the
intensity and tempo of the practice session. If you continually condition

your players at high intensity following a rigorous practice, eventually your team will become overtrained and sluggish. Morale will decrease and injuries may occur. In this example, Monday and Tuesday are hard days. Wednesday is a light, low-intensity jog to recover from the previous workouts, and Thursday's medium-intensity run will be enough even though players do no conditioning before the practice game on Saturday. The athletes will get some conditioning by playing on Saturday, so they need no postgame conditioning.

Weight Training

Players should continue weight training all year. Although the emphasis in the preseason shifts toward skills and strategies, other components remain important. Weight training should be done at the end of the day so that players can give all their energy to the practice session. Because the athletes will be fatigued at the end of the day, workouts should be short so that athletes can achieve higher intensity. In the example, the weight workouts occur on four separate days, one day for each part of the body—chest, back, legs, arms. After a 90-minute practice session, the athletes will find it much easier to prepare mentally for only 10 to 15 minutes of hard work rather than the 30 to 45 minutes of a regular workout.

IN-SEASON TRAINING

In-season training is designed to maintain the fitness, strength, and speed gains achieved during the off- and preseasons. During the in-season the primary emphasis is on skill training. A strength program is still needed to minimize strength loss during the season, but it will need to be modified to accommodate travel and games. Too much weight training combined with weekly games puts athletes at risk for injury and burnout. You can use a training schedule like the one that follows throughout the in-season, which usually lasts about 16 weeks. The first example includes matches on Wednesday and Saturday. We have provided two other examples of in-season training weeks to illustrate how you might accommodate different game schedules.

IN-SEASON

Monday

Plyometrics—Double standing long jump: 3 × 4 and repeat triple tuck jump: 4 × 4

Conditioning—Stride the length of the pitch and walk the width × 12–15 repetitions

Weight training—Clean pull 3 × 3; leg extension 2 × 20; and leg curl 5 × 5

Tuesday

Plyometrics—None

Conditioning—None the day before a match

Weight training—Lat pulldown 5 × 5 and seated row 5 × 5

Wednesday

Soccer match

Thursday

Plyometrics—None

Conditioning—Substitutes who saw limited playing time only, stride 8 × 100 yards (91 meters) with 24-second intervals, 1-minute rest; 8 × 80 yards (73 meters) with 18-second intervals, 1-minute rest; 8 × 60 yards (55 meters) with 12-second intervals, 3-minute rest; and sprint 10 × 10 yards (9 meters) with 10-second intervals

Weight training—Incline press 3 × 5 and military press 3 × 5

Friday

Plyometrics—Vertical jump to a standing long jump: 4 × 5 and side to side, one-legged, one cone: 3 × 10

Conditioning—None the day before a match

Weight training—Triceps pushdown 4 × 8 and barbell curl 3 × 8

Saturday

Soccer match

Sunday

Plyometrics—None

Conditioning—Substitutes who saw limited playing time only, 2×100 yards (91 meters) with 30-second intervals; 2×80 yards (73 meters) with 24-second intervals; 2×60 yards (55 meters) with 18-second intervals; 2×40 yards (37 meters) with 12-second intervals; 2×20 yards (18 meters) with 6-second intervals 2-minute rest; 2×20 yards (18 meters) with 6-second intervals; 2×40 yards (37 meters) with 12-second intervals; 2×60 yards (55 meters) with 18-second intervals; 2×80 yards (73 meters) with 24 second-intervals; and 2×100 yards (91 meters) with 30-second intervals

Weight training—Makeup day

Summary

Warm-Up and Flexibility

As in the preseason, players perform warm-up and flexibility training before practice sessions during the season. Because agility training, plyometrics, conditioning, and weight training will be part of the daily practice schedule, a separate warm-up and flexibility session is not necessary.

Agility

Players perform all agility drills with a ball as part of the daily practice schedule. The coach can choose the drills based on what he or she feels the players need to work on. This could mean dribbling through an obstacle course, running through a series of cones and coming on to the ball to shoot or receive a pass, or other kinds of drills.

Plyometrics

A good training effect results from plyometrics performed twice per week. Keeping the drills simple yet explosive and employing low volume is the best formula for keeping athletes at peak power.

Conditioning

Full-time players will get nearly all the conditioning they need by playing in matches. Determining whether a full-time player fatigues because of too much conditioning or too little can be discovered only by trial and error, taking into consideration the amount of playing time the player receives, the level of activity the player experiences during a match, and the energy level of the player in the training sessions leading up to the matches. In a Wednesday-Saturday match schedule, players have three days before the first match and only two days before the second, so it is difficult to condition the full-time players and give them a full day off before the second match. Having only one day of conditioning for the entire team seems not nearly enough until you consider that the practice sessions can serve as conditioning.

Weight Training

During this period, as during any other, weight training is as important as other components. All the components work together to form a year-round program. The only thing that changes is the emphasis. The goal during in-season training is to hold on to as much strength as possible for speed, endurance, power, and most important, to reduce risk of injury. Never settle for the maintenance of strength. If an athlete can increase strength during the season, go for it! But weight training must not hinder performance by causing fatigue or by taking time away from practicing skills. Constant modification of the training menu may be necessary to accommodate time constraints, travel, amount of playing time, or injury. The athlete should train his whole body in seven days. The player should study the schedule of the upcoming week and try to repeat the cycle in seven days. Training one body part per day allows the athlete to train without sacrificing intensity or quality. If an athlete's menu is short, it is possible to train more than one body part per session. The idea is to reduce the time spent in the weight room and raise the intensity of the training session. Athletes who play a large portion of a match should not weight train afterward because match fatigue will minimize the training effect. Substitute players, however, may be able to complete their training responsibility that day, depending on the team's schedule following a match.

IN-SEASON

Alternative Schedule A
(One Weekend Match)

Monday
Conditioning—Heavy
Weight training—Chest, shoulders

Tuesday

Plyometrics—Vertical and horizontal

Conditioning—Light

Weight training—Back, arms

Wednesday

Conditioning—Heavy

Weight training—Legs

Thursday

Plyometrics—Lateral and vertical

Conditioning—Light

Weight training—Makeup day

Friday

Conditioning—Medium conditioning, if any, for the substitutes only

Weight training—None

Saturday

Match

Sunday

Conditioning—None

Weight training—Makeup day

IN-SEASON

Alternative Schedule B
(Two Weekend Matches)

Monday

Plyometrics—Vertical and lateral

Conditioning—Medium

Weight training—Chest, shoulders

Tuesday
Conditioning—Heavy
Weight training—Back, arms

Wednesday
Plyometrics—Lateral and horizontal
Conditioning—Light
Weight training—Legs

Thursday
Conditioning—Light for full-time players, heavy for substitutes
Weight training—Makeup day

Friday
Match

Saturday
Light practice session

Sunday
Match

Although the basic examples shown are based on a collegiate season, the programs maintain their relevance to other types of seasons as well. Preseason and in-season training formats remain the same regardless of the length of those competitive periods. Slight adjustments must be made for those athletes involved in both school and club teams because their competitive season is longer. This can infringe on the important developmental period.

ABOUT THE AUTHORS

Named the head coach of the Los Angeles Galaxy in 1999, **Sigi Schmid** led the Galaxy to the final round of the Major League Soccer playoffs that same year and into the MLS semifinals in 2000 and 2001. These accomplishments only add to Schmid's long and impressive record of success in competitive soccer.

Before becoming coach of the L.A. Galaxy, Schmid served as head soccer coach for the University of California at Los Angeles (UCLA). His 21 years with the university were marked by an outstanding winning record of 322-63-33, 16 consecutive postseason appearances, and three NCAA Division I championships.

An assistant on Bora Milutinovic's 1994 World Cup coaching staff, Schmid was appointed the coach of the U.S. Under-20 national team in 1998. He guided the team through CONCACAF qualifying rounds and into the FIFA World Youth Championships.

A successful player before becoming a coach, Schmid was a starter at midfield for the UCLA Bruins from 1972 to 1975. His long standing commitment to the game was honored in 1996 when he was inducted into the National Soccer Hall of Fame as one of the first members of the American Youth Soccer Organization. Schmid currently resides in Torrance, California.

Bob Alejo has more than 20 years of experience in college and professional sports. As the former strength and conditioning coach for the Oakland Athletics, he was responsible for designing and implementing a year-round fitness program for the baseball organization, which consists of nutrition, flexibility, warm-up, conditioning, strength training, and rehabilitation.

Before joining the Athletics, Alejo served as the interim strength and conditioning coach for the 1994 World Cup soccer team. He helped to develop the warm-up, flexibility, conditioning, and strength programming in coordination with the sports medicine and coaching staff of the U.S. Men's National Soccer Team.

Currently an executive board member of the Professional Baseball Strength and Conditioning Coaches Society and a member of USA Volleyball Sports Medicine and Performance Commission, Alejo has also worked as conditioning coach and facility administrator at UCLA from 1990 to 1993, as well as head conditioning coach and assistant conditioning coach from 1984 to 1990. During this time he directed and supervised the fitness programs of 21 men's and women's intercollegiate sports. Before this he was program coordinator and strength and conditioning coordinator at the Sports Medicine and Training Center in Chico, California; and head conditioning coach for football at California State University, Chico.

The author of the *Oakland Athletics Winter Conditioning Manual*, Alejo has also co-authored 6 books and more than 50 articles for major sports publications. Alejo graduated from California State University with a degree in physical education. He currently resides in San Ramon, California.

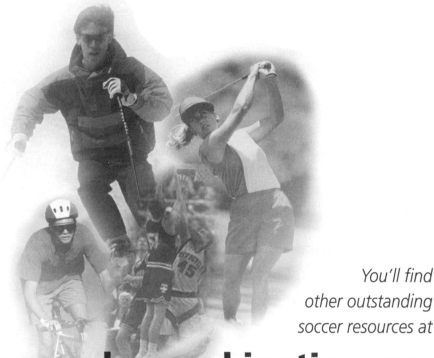